Fast Start in Property Management

Tips & Tactics for Light Commercial Buildings

Karl Breckenridge

Real Estate
Education Company
a division of Dearborn Financial Publishing, Inc.

While a great deal of care has been taken to provide accurate and current information, the ideas, suggestions, general principles and conclusions presented in this book are subject to local, state and federal laws and regulations, court cases and any revisions of same. The reader is thus urged to consult legal counsel regarding any points of law—this publication should not be used as a substitute for competent legal advice.

Publisher: Kathleen A. Welton
Acquisitions Editor: Patrick J. Hogan
Associate Editor: Karen A. Christensen
Project Editor: Linda S. Miller
Cover Design: Sam Concialdi

Printed in the United States of America.

91 92 93 10 9 8 7 6 5 4 3 2 1

Library of Congress Cataloging-in-Publication Data

Breckenridge, Karl.
    Fast start in property management : tips and tactics in light commercial buildings / Karl Breckenridge.
        p.   cm.
    Includes index.
    ISBN 0-79310-257-X : $19.95
    1. Real estate management.   2. Building management.   3. Commercial buildings—Management.   I. Title.
    HD1394.B74 1991
    647'.962—dc20

                                                                90-25989
                                                                CIP

Dedication

To Don and Dan Stockwell:
their twinstantaneous wit keeps us smilin'...

To Ted Stoever, CPM:
old lessors never die,
they just exercise their last option...

Contents

Preface

On two or three Saturday afternoons each year, we stroll the four-block length of Petaluma's main street. "Peggy Sue Got Married" in Petaluma (on the north tip of the San Francisco Bay); but many years before those Hollywood nuptials were spoken, we snuck downtown and peeked into the toy store while mom and dad visited with grandma.

Then, as now, the little town was considered "quaint," and now, 40 years later, we're prepared to offer a definition of quaint: *Quaint* is *no shopping centers*, just a succession of retail stores, each with its own sign out front and its own storefront windows and doorway onto a sidewalk. (We'd like to include a '34 Ford panel truck parked diagonally in front, with a replica of RCA's "Nipper Hearing His Master's Voice" painted on the body, but that might be taking things too far.)

And *quaint* is the office over each of these stores, with the proprietor's name in gold leaf on the window. Or an office wedged between the soda fountain with the checkerboard floor and the milliner with the French name on its hatboxes. This office should have a big, perpetually terminal fern in the window, black-wrought fly fans, a dim *belle-époque* light fixture over a lady with a postiche working a mahogany pullwire PBX board and a Chevrolet businessman's coupe out in front next to Nipper.

*   *   *   *

The realities of the '90s have pummeled *quaint* into a heartless bean-counter's Rorschach blot on a spreadsheet and moved the milliner and the fountain into a mall, or at the very least into a strip center. Their logos had to be redesigned to fit on the 40-inch fascia over all the stores—Nipper and the Chevy coupe are long gone. And an office will only grudgingly be allowed between them.

Most offices are way down the street in a building with one off-street parking spot for every 250 square feet of office space, two-by-four-foot fluorescent fixtures at nine-foot ceiling height, projecting 100 foot-candles of light to a 30-inch-high desktop, a carpet with a UL-rated flame-spread rate—and, in place of the fly fan, a Honeywell climate-control system monitored in Atlanta by satellite telemetry. The BMW coupe outside has a phone and a fax!

*   *   *   *

This book is of retail and office building management. In Peggy Sue's Petaluma, and every similar Main Street U.S.A., the proprietors took care of their own buildings—they called the roofer and the locksmith, the sign painter and the plumber. They shoveled their own snow (but of course *not* in Petaluma!), and they swept up shop on Fridays. Their insurance policies were a maximum of three pages long, and they had at least one brass soda-ash fire extinguisher in each store to pacify the fire department (which, by the way, still had a Dalmatian).

Time has marched on. The bywords of contemporary management are *cooperation* and *communication* among a number of occupants—the fusing together of many businesses under one roof, with one front door and address, but with different hours and days of business operation and a common desire to carve their chunk of autonomy out of an economic system that mandates a multiplicity of neighbors.

Our job is to make these tenants comfortable while maximizing the property ownership benefit to our clients. A few tricks of the trade are coming around the corner now—written for the real estate professional involved in property management, or for the owner of one of these small buildings.

*   *   *   *

And if you visit a little town like Petaluma, you'll probably share our hope that some main streets should forever have a '34 Ford panel truck parked in front of a soda fountain, and that none of us will ever be called upon to open a new mall or manage a high-rise office there!

Karl Breckenridge
March 1991

Introduction

Once upon a time we managed a 19,000-square-foot building owned by our family (which in and of itself is a foolish endeavor, but that's not significant to this anecdote). One morning we drove to the building and observed two nuns in the parking lot, in the company of a fire crew whose Reno fire engine was parked nearby. They were all seven congregated over a fairly good-sized lion cub on a leash, at the other end of which was an employee of the building tenant.

If there is a scintilla of worthwhile information to be gleaned from the rest of this book, it is this: As building managers, we will find times when our presence, skills and judgment are beneficial to a situation. We will also learn to recognize occasions when we are best off to stay in our cars and drive on, possibly to hear more about the occurrence at a later time—or possibly not.

On that morning, we changed lanes and kept going.

*   *   *   *

We learned later, in the comparative sanity of our own office, that the fire engine was merely making a routine inspection tour of a Hartford Insurance office when the Dominican sisters from St. Mary's Hospital visited the claims department to complete some forms for a patient insured by the Hartford Stag. A Hartford employee's declawed lion cub was merely an exhibit for an impromptu grownup show-and-tell day. Our point: There's an explanation for everything where rental buildings are concerned, but often *mañana* is quite soon enough to find out.

(The lion cub, we're told, has long since grown to a proud monarch and been shipped off to a zoo.)

The Property Manager

The following pages are aimed at the property manager. Square in our sights is the owner of a small building or a real estate professional licensed by some state to act "for others and for compensation," the benchmark of a licensed property manager with a fiduciary relationship to a property owner. In the usual scheme of things, this professional has executed with a fiduciary principal an "employment contract," stating in quite certain terms:

1. the scope of the agent's responsibility,
2. the duration of time for which the employment will last, and
3. the method by which the agent will be compensated.

The three criteria above are the first of several gross oversimplifications you will encounter in this text (and we'll try to highlight all of them as we move along).

Contracts.   We're quick to point out that if you're assuming management from another agent, you should be exonerated from the errors and omissions that you inherited from that agent. That is one of the more important elements of a well-defined employment contract, and at this juncture, we'll offer a one-time plug for our favorite club, the National Association of REALTORS®, which numbers among its affiliates the Institute of Real Estate Management, known more colloquially as IREM.

IREM has perfected a dandy management contract, which is only one of a myriad of reasons for becoming involved in IREM if you're interested in management on a full-time and long-term basis. We'll not become a cheerleader for the Institute here, but we will point out that the *Certified Property Manager* (CPM) designation is frequently demanded by lenders for managers supervising the lender's portfolio properties, and in many cases the lender will seek an *Accredited Management Office* (AMO) to handle their properties. Enough said here—contact the branch in your town, usually through your local Board of REALTORS®, for more information.

Licensure.   Our manager has possibly a small, one-person operation for which he or she fulfills most of the duties alone, or with the help of one or two other people in the office. The big national real estate management firms have an entire floor of engineers to handle fire sprinkler systems and another of landscape architects. This book is for simple folks—we do it all!

Leasing is an integral part of our duties, and we'll devote a later segment of this book to that function. This book is not a pretender to the title of an all-inclusive leasing text, as those books exist already in excellent, readable form. What we will do is relate information in those leasing textbooks with the sticks and stones within the physical plant demised in the lease. (The first portion of the book is devoted more to the physical side of the property. Once we've expanded on that, we can address leasing more coherently.)

We note that, in a few states, a person may practice property management without a real estate license. But the states are unanimous in the opinion that leasing constitutes an effort to convey an interest in real property. And, in witness of that opinion, we can state with 99 percent accuracy that a person engaged in leasing falls within the real estate licensing acts of the states.

And: The several states also agree that the location (situs) of the managed property, not the domicile of the managing agency, determines the state of jurisdiction.

The Building

A common barometer used in defining the size of commercial properties is the *gross leasable area,* or more commonly just *GLA.* But we won't be using that term at this stage of the text. In the interest of graphic examples we'll describe the buildings that this book is best suited for, and charge you, the reader, with the responsibility of locating a real, existing building in your area, then keeping that building in your mind's eye as you move through these pages. It's not our intention to convert you into a qualified building contractor or architect;

but a minimal knowledge of construction and design is a requisite to property management.

For a prototype office building, find a local structure two or three stories high with 6,000 to 10,000 square feet per floor, a basement, an elevator and a generous parking lot. We'll look at sprinklers and alarms, so include them. Heating and air conditioning are important, and shall hereinafter be expressed as *HVAC*—heating, ventilating and air conditioning (or occasionally as just *air handling*). A multitenant building would be ideal, so we can settle a few hypothetical inter-tenant squabbles about parking, signs and HVAC.

And for the retail center example, a little strip center with a dozen or so retail tenancies will do nicely, with at least one that remains open until late evening; one with special plumbing needs, such as a laundromat; one that creates a lot of trash that overflows a dumpster; another that generates frequent vehicle trips and eats up all the park-ing. And somewhere in the middle is a nonretail tenant like an All-state agent trying to get some work done in the eye of this retail hurricane. *That's* a center we can learn something from!

*   *   *   *

So drive around your town and find two properties that meet the above guidelines. Park and roam around them for a little while; stop in to see the inside of an office or a retail store. By the time you read the closing pages of this book, all the tenants will know your car and will have something pleasant to say to you. You'll know every valve in the mechanical room, which lamp is burned out in the parking lot (and how much higher it is than the top step on your ladder) and why you keep on driving when the firemen are playing with the lion cub. You will be known by all—as the property manager!

The Epilogue to the Prologue

We learned early in this property-management effort that occasionally the flow of a chapter requires touching on a topic whose full explana-tion belongs later in the text. Consequently we seem to do some hop-scotching around and may use a term several times, with scant explanation, before arriving at that point in the text where we want to land on it firmly with both boots and fully explain it. We ask the reader's forbearance—if it's important, we *will* get to it. To paraphrase the famous vintner: We will explain no word before its time.

A second and minor dilemma is that we are aligning the content to both retail and office occupancies. In reducing both occupancies to their skeletal forms, we find a lease is a lease and a building is a building, and most words hold true for either. In cases where a significant difference in tenancies merits an explanation in the text, we'll highlight that difference.

*   *   *   *

So off now we go, to unlock the door to property management—appropriately, with a chapter devoted to access!

1

Access and Keys

There are in our industry two types of property managers: Those who have locked themselves out of a building, and those who are going to lock themselves out of a building. For this reason, most of us have a secret "doomsday" key somewhere around our properties to provide some kind of access in a worst-case situation. A good friend hid such a key on a ledge inside a sprinkler irrigation box below a planter. One summer night she had occasion to use it.

She recalls now that the bite of a black widow spider is not terribly painful. But several minutes later when cyanosis set in and her fingernails turned blue, she found it quite easy to forget that she only went by the building to use a telephone, and that sometimes other managerial activities, like breathing, must take priority.

Presumably both these ladies survived, our friend to manage another day and the widow to continue devouring mates and managers. And presumably the key has been moved to less hostile environs.

*　*　*　*

Possibly we just inadvertently blew a secret of building managers from Malibu to Maine: Just as residential keys hide on top of a porchlight, commercial keys hide in valve and circuit-breaker boxes. But not being prone to cry over spilt milk, we'll move along to a chapter with *access* as our "key" word, for if we're going to manage them, we have to get inside them, just as our tenants do.

Not all those entitled to enter one group of doors in the building are entitled to pass through another group; in the same vein, some are welcome to enter during business hours but are denied access after hours and on the weekend. Indeed, we the managers ourselves don't have, or want, free run in certain buildings. In this chapter we'll sort out and try to consolidate the number of keys we must haul around (and potentially lose).

*   *   *   *

We need to classify levels of entry, and we'll use three categories, with some inevitable spilling over from one to another. The first level includes our tenants, numerically one or more. The second is building ownership, management and maintenance. A final broad level is emergency personnel, most frequently a fire company, not blessed with a lot of time to get into the building, but get in they will, with a Schlage key or a McCulloch chain saw. (And it's far easier to lock up after the crew that has a key.)

The technology that (in simplest terms) keeps Tenant A from going into Tenant B's office, keeps both of them from stealing the Owner's janitorial supplies, yet admits them both into the tenants' lounge, has turned into a multimillion-dollar industry. But at the root of it all is the one little gadget that we all carry in our purses or pockets—a door key.

The Key

Not much can be said about a lone key, but as the atom that the whole managerial molecular chain builds on, it deserves a little attention. We'll proceed then in no particular order, but with some ''key'' points to ponder:

One point is the quality of the material from which we make our keys. Factory keys are usually substantial, but there are some low-budget blanks in the marketplace that pose difficulties of reliability when duplicates are ground, or that have short lives with repeated use. In cold climates, a door key is more akin to a wrench when turning a cold lockset—the budget blanks occasionally snap off in the keyway.

Regrettably, one of the niftiest products on the key scene fails in this category: The aluminum blanks available in bright colors, making one key easy to spot in a ring. The color's great, but the soft material gives us consistent problems. A good alternative is a colored plastic band that slips over the head of a key. They thicken a key ring but make frequently used keys easy to spot in the dark.

"Do Not Duplicate."   You'll hear two schools of thought about a stamp that most locksmiths can put on our replacement keys: DO NOT DUPLICATE. One school discounts the effectiveness of the stamp; those naysayers claim if a person wants a key duplicated, someone will cut it. And they're right.

However, the average employee of a tenant in your office building seldom has a ready pipeline to a person with a key machine, with the appropriate blank (of which there are probably a thousand variations) and with a mindset to ignore the "DND" notation. All three elements are necessary, and it's usually a little more trouble than it's worth.

A reputable locksmith won't touch a key with the warning; in fact, we've become involved in properties where the prior managers so designated some keys, and we had to provide a letter from the owner to the locksmith approving the duplication. We're told that trade associations and bonding companies occasionally send people into the field, attempting to secure copies of such keys, entrapping unscrupulous locksmiths.

We'll take our chances handing out "DND" keys—if we require a higher degree of security, we'll use a specialty lockset. The text will turn to those in a few pages.

Key Tagging.   Serious building managers should make two stops early in their careers: At the stationers for a box of cardboard key tags, and at the hardware store (or a key shop) for a set of nine steel dies, numbered 1 through 0 and sold in a little wooden box. For those readers who weren't math majors, we note that a 6 may be used as a 9, and if that concept still needs explanation, we nominate that reader for the next continuing-education math course.

The Eleventh Commandment in property management is to tag each and every key that ever comes into your possession while you can remember what it fits. The corollary is that you never give a person a key without tagging it, for fear of (a) that person forgetting what it fits, and (b) a person having the right key without knowing it and hitting you up for another.

The tags and the dies further that effort. A tag can fall off, but a die-stamped number, rendered with a smart tap of a hammer, is forever. We have keys that we stamped back in the 1960s, still in use.

And how do we stamp it? Seldom with a number that would tell a bad guy what it fits, in case someone in the management system loses a key ring. Entire homes and buildings have been rekeyed in response to those situations. We'll share our code with you, with the knowledge that if we lose our key ring now a code that has worked since 1966 will be in every bookstore in the country: The first digit in an address goes last, e.g., 1645 Vassar Street is stamped 6451. Simple. We're less worried about the interior of a building; in those cases we usually punch a couple of insignificant extra numbers on the key: room 201 is marked 42201, or 24201.

Now let's all agree not to use the same system. Find one that works for you, and use it consistently.

The Key Cabinet.   Somewhere in your growing organization you'll want to start a central location for keys, and an attractive lockable key cabinet fills the bill. These aren't cheap, but get the one that's two sizes bigger than you think you'll need, and you'll probably wind up filling it.

The preceding comments about key identification hold true; and it's not a bad idea to keep the index separate from the cabinet.

Minor Note: As much as practicable, it's best to keep the *original* key that came with a lockset in the cabinet, and use it to produce other keys as necessary. Copies of copies of originals start losing their tolerance somewhere in the third or fourth generation and become difficult to work in the keyway.

Construction Locks

Now and then we all have the pleasure of taking over a brand-new project—office or retail center—to tread where no manager has gone before us. On such an assignment, or in an older structure following a remodelling, you may encounter a "construction lockset."

Quite briefly, these sets are delivered as a group to the site by the lock manufacturer, and knobs are installed at random on each lockable door of an office building, for example. All the knobs may be locked each evening, but the construction workers can open them all with the construction key, facilitating their efforts.

At the time a tenant takes occupancy, he or she is given a key to the leased space that arrived from the factory in a sealed packet—no duplicates. That key is inserted in the lockset and turned, fairly hard, and it cuts its own unique path through the tumblers. From that turn on, no other key—including the construction key—will open the lockset.

The tenant may then make keys to her or his heart's delight, secure in the knowledge that no one else has access. A side benefit is that you are absolved of the potential liability arising out of a key floating around in the wrong hands.

A Master System

We asked the reader to locate a 12-unit retail center for use as an example from time to time, and such a time has arrived: Our challenge is that we are the owners or managers of this little strip center and would like to have emergency access to each of the 12 spaces, plus the fire sprinkler riser room and the storage room.

A slight digression is necessary: Most tenants have no problem with management access, if the request is properly couched in reasonable terms. We'll offer a way in a few pages to overcome a significant objection, and we note that there are some tenancies we'd just as soon not have access to.

One option is to carry 13 keys (riser and storage rooms keyed alike), and mark them all by address per your personal coding. A better option is a *master* system—one key opens all the locks. The tenants all have separate keys to their own stores, but the master key has a tiny extra or altered notch that lifts one or two tumblers an iota higher and allows the keyway to turn.

The master system works equally well in the office setting—a master on the front and side exterior doors, janitor closet, riser room, supply closets (or any ''house'' door) and each office within the building.

On systems from some manufacturers, the same master keyway can be carried over to a padlock, for a dumpster or parking lot chain. Or, it may be compatible with an electric switch or to turn on a gate arm on a parking lot or HVAC equipment after a weekend.

We're sensitive about who gets the master keys. They come to us from the factory sealed, separate from the lockset shipments. They're not marked. And we'd be more inclined to give maintenance labor a ring of 12 keys (for the above retail center) than a master key.

*   *   *   *

Also available from a few major local manufacturers, and stopping short of the mindbending exotic systems, is a *grandmaster* system—a master with an added hierarchy. Example: In our office building, imagine a suite of three private offices within one tenant's demised premises—we'll call it Mr. Dithers's suite, to keep this straight. Each of those three offices is keyed differently, to accommodate the privacy of the executive within. We know that a master key can be provided to permit Mr. Dithers access to the front door of his suite and each of his separate offices.

But we don't want to grant Mr. Dithers access to the suite across the hall, nor do we want to start having suites go off the master system with a resulting growth of our key ring. So we go to a grandmaster system: The dominant key (the *grandmaster*) opens every lock in the building—we alone have that one. The *master* works the sets in a group, in our example the three offices in the Dithers suite—that's carried by Mr. Dithers. (There's a different master key for each tenant.) And an *individual* key opens the door to Dithers's suite and only one interior office. Needless to say, that key is Dagwood's.

Keypad Systems

Keypads are real dandies for regulating access to an area where a relatively large number of people have need to enter, but quite possibly with frequent changes in the people or their need for access. Rekeying the door and supplying all those who are still welcome with a new key could turn into a full-time job.

For these situations, we suggest to our tenants the installation of a keypad system, which may be electrical or mechanical, but similar in operation: A series of buttons akin to a TouchTone® phone are pressed in sequence to open a door—on some models, an attempt at a second or third incorrect sequence sounds an alarm.

Management, when the need exists (often in response to a terminated employee or from just plain too many employees sharing the code verbally with unauthorized people), can open the lock with a key, reset a new code sequence and restart the appropriate employees off on the right foot. (By the way, outside the realm of office and retail buildings, these are great for apartment and condo swimming pools, as no key is required and you can change them daily if necessary.)

And concluding the keypad paragraphs, we'll recall that we blew the secret of most property managers by disclosing our frequent tendency to hide a key in a breaker cabinet or the irrigation box. For the smug among you who use keypads on your offices, we'll reveal the results of a study taken by the Breckenridge Institute in 1982 that 84 percent of all keypads, briefcases and Lincoln Continentals can be opened with the last four digits of the owner's Social Security number, or my name isn't 7764.

Card Entry

A high-tech extension of the keypad system is a magnetic card reader, set in a slot adjoining selected doors. An employee, issued an appropriate card similar to a credit card, uses that in lieu of a key. In addition to the capability of instantaneously denying access to unauthorized individuals, these systems, often placed on both sides of a latched door, can store and retrieve the time of the comings and goings of employees.

A good friend of ours in Reno works in a high-security building with 16 "cells" created within his office by spring-closer doors controlled by mag cards. Not only is the news of his migration about the office constantly transmitted to his company's district office in San Francisco by satellite, a locator screen in the receptionist's station highlights his present location—and, we suspect, his course, altitude and fuel load.

As building managers, we'll seldom be confronted by our tenants' weird and wonderful notions about security *within* their space, but we will from time to time be expected to cooperate when these notions involve access from the exterior to the common area within the building. And yes, we expect to be reminded by a reader that the human voice, cornea and hand bone structure are also the basis of refined entry-limiting devices. We'll remind that reader of the statement that we're simple folks managing modest buildings, and leave the aerospace and defense I.D. systems to others.

Special Access and Security Needs

After-Hours Activity. Notwithstanding some of the overkill that some of our tenants conjure up to squeeze the last drop of security and level of access out of the master and keypad systems cited above, it's occasionally indicated that a building should be locked, period. For these occasions we offer the alternative of a deadbolt installed on the same door as a mastered system, but with the ultimate lockset: a key in your pocket alone. In many leases, entry of a building by a tenant after a certain hour of the evening or on a weekend or at least on Sunday is precluded by the lease. The deadbolt is a good way to override whatever system is in use in the knob lockset.

Some care must be taken here to assure that a fire exit will not be violated when stragglers are still in the building. In a similar vein, we endorse a handle on the inside of a door permitting the door to be opened without a key, after the lockset on the door has been closed for the evening. Absent this handle, we could inadvertently confine a person inside the building for the night.

Elevator Floor Restriction.   It's not uncommon in this space-hungry age for an architect to eliminate the traditional elevator lobby of old, and simply have the elevator doors open into the tenant's premises, if those tenants have exclusive use of the whole floor.

To accommodate such tenants we install a key-operated electrical lock in the elevator cars. In the "normal" position a visitor can dispatch the car to that floor with the button in the car. On weekends or evenings, when the switch is "locked," only those with a key may visit that floor.

This configuration is of minor importance to us as building managers, as long as we regard the elevator lock as just another variation of locking a tenant's front door and subject that lock to the same cautions and procedures.

Minor Note: The fire department can override the lockout if necessary, and a person on the restricted floor can call the elevator to that floor in most instances.

The Knox System. Our final method of getting from the outside to the inside of your building, office, or retail center is a key that neither love nor money can buy. It is probably the best-regulated civilian key system in America: the Knox system.

In practice, the majority of us who arrived in commercial management through the residential brokerage system will detect a vast similarity to the good old lockbox—the same size, just a hundred times tougher and with better key control. In a nutshell, we put a Knox box on the side of a building, usually over an entry door or a riser room door, and place the key to that door into the box. An arriving firefighter opens the Knox box with the Knox key on the fire engine, extracts the building key and enters the building to do whatever's necessary.

Now for the nitty gritty: You can't buy the box. You give a check payable to the Knox Company to your local fire department, who actually places the order. The Knox Company in Southern California sends the box to you, the building manager.

When it arrives, you mount it, usually more than eight feet above the pavement, and proximate to the desired door. After the box is mounted, you call the firehouse and a big, red fire engine will drive to your building. You give the crew a key to the door, they put that key into the box, replace the lid and lock the box with the key carried on the engine. From that event forward, they can enter the building without tearing up the place.

* * * *

The reference to the fire engine is significant: The fire inspectors' and staff cars don't carry a Knox key—they're all over town all day. But just as the big rigs' movements are recorded, so are the movements of the Knox keys. Obviously the key is safe—it's usually on a ring about a foot in diameter, and its presence on each engine or truck is verified at each shift change. They don't loan it out. A fire company responds to situations when police and ambulance personnel need entry. And the Knox Company doesn't exactly have a welcome mat out—they hold in an unknown location a key to half the locks in America.

Extensions of the system are Knox padlocks and switches, operated by the same key carried on the fire engine. You'll find these, for example, on an electrically operated entry gate: The Knox keyswitch opens the gate if the power's on—during an outage, the unlocked padlock allows the gate to swing free and admit the emergency vehicle.

We would urge managers of buildings of any significant complexity or expanse to investigate the Knox entry system if it's in place in your community.

High-Security Locks.   In the early segment of the chapter we alluded to higher-security lock systems, and they naturally follow in the wake of the Knox system—many of their characteristics are similar.

Readers of our prior books know of our disdain for endorsing products, unless compelling reason exists. And in this chapter about access, locksmiths would probably agree that we'd be remiss in omitting a reference to Medeco, Abloy and Best systems.

These locks share many traits: They are all three made of extremely tough alloys and are quite damage-resistant; their keys are controlled, and blanks are unavailable except by mail order through bonded locksmiths (who don't keep them on premises); finally, the keys, when shipped from the factory, can't be cut on conventional machines—the teeth have a distinct "signature."

These products are available as conventional knob locksets, deadbolts and padlocks. They're tough and expensive and do the job. As a practical matter, you probably wouldn't use these locks exclusively in a building with normal tenants, for the simple reason that key duplication and rekeying, an ongoing function of management, becomes an unnecessarily burdensome task. But if a higher level of security is desired by a tenant, these are the products that do the job.

Some Housekeeping Pointers

And if You Don't Want Access.   A short housekeeping pointer, left over from the paragraph about handling the tenant who didn't want to give access to the lessor or manager (and conversely, if you want to be in a position to prove that you *haven't* entered a demised premises):

Ask that tenant to tape a door key to a sheet of paper and put it into a sealed envelope (and not an envelope with a business name on it).

Have the tenant sign that envelope so that it's unique, one that you can't replace with a substitute. Then you mark the tenant's address on the envelope (coded), and keep it where you can find it in a hurry.

At any juncture, you may show that the envelope's intact, proof that you haven't toured the premises without the tenant's consent. But if you need in, as in immediately, you've got your key.

We frequently encounter such a situation, about fifty-fifty by the tenant's initiation or by our own. This little stratagem usually conquers the resistance.

Open Padlocks.　When you unlock a padlocked area, don't leave the lock hanging open—relock it around the fence webbing or hasp or a chain link. Bad guys look for open locks and have been known to replace them with a similar lock that they have a key for. Unaware of the switch, we replace their lock at night, and they are then at liberty to come in and browse around.

(High-security locks usually require the shackle to be closed before the key can be withdrawn.)

Consult a Locksmith.　We're hesitant to use the word *pick* in a chapter dealing with locks, but we'll offer the advice to pick a locksmith you get along easily with, familiarize him or her with your needs and don't be afraid to seek counsel. We've been locking ourselves out of other people's buildings for two decades and are still learning of new or improved products we could have trapped ourselves with.

One slick service of a local 'smith that we've used for many years is a repository of our keys on their premises, stamped to correspond with the code in our office. If we need three keys, they cut them, stamp them and drop them off. And if that tenant moves out they can rekey a cylinder, make a few keys and install it in one trip. (And if they're the charitable sort, have them show you how to remove a Schlage cylinder or invert a keyway, and save themselves a trip that frequently isn't worth their gas!)

*　*　*　*

An Observation, in Closing: Show us a property manager, and we'll show you someone the left side of whose brain won't energize the right arm to latch a door shut until it senses a set of keys being held in the left hand!

2

The Building, Part I

There once was an enclosed retail mall so monumentally doomed to economic failure that the owners decided to demolish it. But the wrecking crew got a head start, Hollywood-style.

Space on mock storefronts was sold to national merchants for their signs and the vacant mall was lit up and populated like any good mall should be on a Friday night. Then Jake and Elwood led half the police cars in Cook County on a merry chase through Walgreen's Drug via the 7-Eleven market.

Afterward, property managers the nation around beamed and reached for their phones to call the movie producers, to offer problem properties of their own, in case there was to be a sequel to ''The Blues Brothers.''

*   *   *   *

In spite of all the tools for maintaining security that we enumerated in the prior chapter, and just as the best-laid plans of mice and such sometime go awry, a door's been left unlocked in our building. Let's use it to get inside and walk around—in this chapter, to look at blueprints and design integrity, the elevators, illumination, air handling and emergency egress. The following chapter continues the journey, visiting other elements of the structure.

We have a manifold purpose in the occasionally tedious and fleetingly vibrant, yet grippingly comprehensive, look at an American commercial building that we'll take in the next few chapters. One reason is that we are paid by the owner and expected to be familiar with the building and to act in his or her stead. In sum, it's our expertise and attention, and no one else's, that spell long-term success or failure of the owner's asset.

A second is a restatement of the first: We are the only entity that sees the totality of the building. A poorly run building could be served by top-flight subcontractors and maintenance people but be on the verge of collapse when the whole system was knit together. We're the choreographers of that maintenance team.

The third reason is that within the pages of this book, we write to include the leasing function as well as the management. We'd prefer not to look like the village idiot when a prospective tenant asks us about the Walker ducting interval, and we've learned from many educational (read *embarrassing!*) moments that the best way to avoid that frustration is to become totally conversant in the buildings we manage. To whet your interest, we'll promise a look at the building, its mechanicals, and its utilities in the next two chapters. And what book written and read in the 1990s would be complete without a chapter about life safety equipment? That topic's also waiting in the wings.

And yes, Walker ducting is on the agenda within the next few pages.

Blueprints

The building started on paper, so that's a good way to open the chapter: Locate the blueprints used for construction. Most owners, even the least responsible, keep a set, but if they're not to be found, the architect can usually reproduce a set. You don't need every sheet, usually only the *elevations*, the *plan view* of each floor and the *site plan*—showing all improvements on the property, buildings and land, together with elevations and drainage. The mechanicals—plumbing, electrical, HVAC and fire sprinklers—usually comprise a second set. Get them if you can, and retain them.

You'll hear the term *as built*—that's exactly what it means: As the building was built, not designed. Invariably the contractors in the field have to depart from the architect's instructions, and they'll record these deviations on the as-built drawings.

Frequently the *specifications* will be rolled up with the blueprints. This binder tells you that the original drinking fountains were

Haws model 12-345 in brushed stainless finish, saving you from having to rise from your easy chair to check one if your plumber is ordering a replacement.

Blueprints, as-builts and specs should be retained in some safe location and guarded like gold.

Tenant Continuity

A well-designed retail center (or office building; we picked a center only arbitrarily) may begin life as a 12-unit center, with Corbin closers on 12 doors, 12 bathrooms with Kohler low-budget commodes, 12 Westinghouse electrical load centers, 12 Lennox rooftop air handlers and—are we making our point? Our service man, carrying one furnace filter, one 20-amp breaker, one flush valve and one door cylinder on his truck can fix any unit on the property.

Over a period of time, our continuity dilutes, as each tenant performs some *TIB* (a new term for the open-book test at the end of the book: *tenant's improvement and betterments*). In truth, we have some controls in our lease, as TIB's require our approval. In the interest of continuity, whenever we have the opportunity to steer a tenant into an improvement using a component consistent with the original used throughout the center, we're making our own job easier in time to come.

Asset Protection

High on our list of priorities is the protection of the physical asset or its design from our tenants, who frequently, with no malice intended, like to change things around a little to suit their needs.

The Roof.   The classic victim is the roof membrane, a sheet of rubber, felt or vinyl that not only has to endure relentless heat and solidifying cold, but also the tenant-added burden of holes punched in it for pipes and wires, vibrating machinery bolted onto it, ducts cut through it and eyebolts screwed to it to support masts and antenna guy wires. (These same tenants may later wonder why it leaks rainwater— frequently into an adjoining tenant's bay. An ill-placed penetration can allow water to drip onto a beam, which may transport it far from the hole before it falls onto the ceiling—the modern North American indoor record is about 43 feet.)

Damage by some tenancies is predictable—look for your new sports-bar tenant to lag-bolt a parabolic TV satellite dish over their space or the yogurt shoppe to install a rooftop refrigeration compressor. Our standard leases give us control over these alternatives. We'd just as soon have our own subcontractors—carpenter and roofer—cut and seal the holes properly as have to go back later and repair interior water damage when the rain hits the tenant's faulty installation.

Tenant Alterations.   Staying in the protection vein, there are minor notes to add about alterations to the interior of the building performed by the tenant. Many are less a matter of physical damage than of building-code violations—blocked fire exits or lights, spring closers removed on mandatory fire-rated doors or obscured sprinkler heads.

One benign little building alteration in our town that escalated to a four-alarm bureaucratic inferno was a mail slot cut through a wall from a lobby to a secretarial station. No big deal, until the wall was determined to be a four-hour fire wall; the minor alteration was likened to wilful endangerment of the lives of half the hundred people in the building.

The Elevator

Our new account's elevator raises several concerns. The first is that your state requires periodic tests of your elevator car and hoist gear—call the state agency and get that ball rolling if the test period is delinquent. And review the maintenance contract, if any, with the elevator repair contractor.

The next item is the freight padding, and where it's kept. Most elevators in small buildings are equipped with lugs to hang padding onto, to protect the car when it's used to haul freight or office furniture. Inventory the padding and make sure it's used when tenants are moving in or out.

Exclusive use of the elevator on the weekend, by the way, for a move in or out, is seldom a problem. The building's closed, and few people are inconvenienced when the elevator is locked on a floor by turning the emergency stop switch off.

Roof Control.   We need to lend out the key for use of the roof of the car to lift larger objects, e.g., an eight-foot sofa that won't fit inside the elevator car.

As the building manager you have two duties here: first, to control the elevator key and give it out when necessary, and second, to show the tenants how to use the roof platform. (Your elevator tech can show *you* how it works!)

Briefly, most elevator cars have a ROOF position on the control panel. Turning the key to that position allows the car to be controlled by buttons on the roof of the car; the car stops with the roof at floor level and the doors can then be opened, allowing long furniture to be transported to or from a floor atop the car.

That operation should be monitored rather closely by building management during a move.

The Emergency Phone.   Most elevator cars have a telephone with ''ring-down'' dialing: The phone automatically dials a number when the receiver comes off the hook. Our job is to make sure someone is on the other end of that phone, night or day, and that the operator has the elevator repair contractor's 24-hour phone number—who, in turn, needs to get into the building to get the person out of the elevator.

In our early days of property management, we took great satisfaction in restoring a dead emergency phone and hooking it up to an answering service, which had the phone number for the elevator service company. One dark night the janitor got himself stuck in the elevator, used the phone in the elevator car to call for help, and it took only about ten minutes for the service man to arrive there.

It took another two hours, however, to get the elevator man inside the building to extricate the janitor. The author, as a possessor of the building key in this daisy chain, was in San Francisco for the weekend. Not unusual.

A Knox system, detailed in the ''Access'' chapter, is a latter-day method to admit an elevator technician into a building under such circumstances. But do be aware of the foibles of the system, and check it out once in a while to see if all your backstops are working.

And don't kid our janitor about that evening. He's still on our team, but he still avoids elevators.

Emergency Capture.   Throughout these pages we strive for tenant communication and training, and this elevator safety feature is one that needs a manager's attention: Most elevators in modern buildings return to a floor, usually the ground floor, when sensors in the building detect heat or flow from a sprinkler or fire hose. (We'll examine those in greater detail in upcoming chapters.)

The responding firefighters carry a key that allows them to command the elevator car to whatever floor is appropriate. (In some jurisdictions a similar key is available in the building in a "Break Glass" cabinet.)

Our involvement as managers is minimal in this procedure, other than to be aware of it and so advise our tenants, to mark the elevator car with a warning not to use the car in case of fire and to alert tenants to vacate the car briefly during alarm or sprinkler flow tests.

Emergency Elevator Power.   You'll read soon of on-premises power in the form of a generator, which in our smaller buildings may or may not be tied to the elevator. If it is, it will usually only energize relays to drop the elevator to the next lower floor and then provide power to open the doors on that floor.

This is grist for tenant education: The on-premises generator won't raise the elevator (usually), but it will prevent building occupants from becoming stranded in the car.

Illumination

As building managers, two of our duties are of paramount importance, but each occasionally aligns onto a collision course with the other: On the one hand, we have a duty to the principal to run the building economically, and on the other the necessity to provide a safe and comfortable environment for the tenants. (The language in this segment is more in tune with an office than a retail center, but some parallels do exist.)

We can economize operation by conserving utility consumption after normal business hours and on the weekends. We'll start with illumination, then move on to heating or cooling.

Night Lighting.   Somewhere on the Weston light meter that you'll need as a building manager is a comfortable and safe balance between full daytime illumination and pitch blackness, and this is where we

For the most part, these Chronotherm®-type switches are in place in our properties, or can and should be retrofitted if single-stage thermostats were original equipment.

In rare cases older heating equipment or separate furnace and air-conditioner units preclude the use of a Chronotherm®, and we may find our old friend of a few paragraphs ago, the seven-day timer, controlling the air handlers.

Amount of Setback: A common fallacy that many building managers make: They let the temperature fall too far in the setback mode, resulting in an inordinate cost to reheat the building. If we want to maintain heat in a range between 68° and 70°, we probably don't want to let the setback temperature fall below, say, 63°. Here are some words to live by: *it's cheaper to maintain heat than restore it.* Translation: it costs more to bring a building back up to 70° on a Monday morning from 60° than it does to keep the building at 63° all weekend.

Setback Overrides: We need a method to override the setback, to accommodate the people working on a Saturday morning or well into an evening. Control manufacturers are aware of this need and most modern controls have a button to move the control to the OCCUPIED setting for some period of time. The system will usually RETARD by itself in a few hours if the departing employees don't retard it manually.

In older systems, often supported by a seven-day time clock, the escapement switch described above may be used to override the setback for some period of time and then return to after-hours load.

Recovery Time: Unlike a light switch, which turns the lights on instantaneously, heat (or air cooling) has a lag time, possibly a couple of hours in a larger building. If you're setting the thermostat to make employees comfy by 8 A.M., you'll probably have to think in terms of 6 A.M. when adjusting the Chronotherm®—unless you're dealing with the very newest types of Chronotherm®, which have an "anticipator" function. With those, you set 8:00 A.M. and it will determine what time to light up the furnaces to get the building up to the desired temperature by 8:00. If you're retrofitting older equipment, ask your furnace contractor to provide anticipator units.

"Heavy" Air.   Refrigerated air, as in air blown over the coil of an air conditioner, is "heavier" and feels colder than untreated air at the same temperature. We set the heat tripper in winter at 68° to make most of the occupants comfortable. (In 1974 the federal-government-mandated temperature was even lower.) But the same occupants are usually comfortable with the cool tripper set at 74° on a summer day. (Alas, a few will want both trippers both at 68°, summer and winter, but we'll guarantee that you can hang meat in an air-conditioned 68° office.)

In Reno's climate and altitude (4,600' MSL), we find that we don't really want the air conditioning set more than 20 degrees below the outside (ambient) temperature. On a beastly hot day, say 98° outside, we'll let the coolers run up to almost 80° in the office and find most people quite comfortable. That range may vary at lower altitudes or at the seacoast.

Readers of our prior books know that we try to give one freebie tip to save the cover price of each book, and here it is: To psychologically cool a building another 5° for free, attach foot-long streamers to the ceiling air outlets. Occupants see them waving around and know that their office must be comfortable. (That's not our idea—the Chinese learned it centuries ago.)

And if you run into a guy that takes his buildings seriously, he'll tell you that the air outlet is known by the cognoscenti as a "pneumostat." In this book for just plain folks, it's still an air outlet.

The Dummy Thermostat.   On a lark, we installed a leftover thermostat in a new building while it was under construction—in truth, just screwed it to the wall with no guard obscuring it. The other five thermostats in the building led somewhere and did something. This placebo just hung there, but it has served a valuable purpose since 1973: In this 100 + employee building, someone is constantly sneaking by that wall and deftly adjusting the setting, then skulking away, made content and more comfortable in the knowledge that they beat the system.

Wet/Dry Bulb Temperatures.   We're saving leases as a chapter unto themselves, but one clause in many leases should probably fall within this HVAC segment.

That clause is one we ignored for a decade without really knowing what it meant, probably because no one else seemed to know, ask—or care, either. The clause reads something like "Lessor shall maintain an interior temperature of ___° *measured by a wet bulb.*"

But one day we were to learn of wet bulbs. We leased a 2,400 square-foot space to State Farm Insurance, and their facilities manager flew in to give the place a once-over.

This gentleman, vaguely reminiscent of the love-child of Roseanne Barr and the Janitor-in-a-Drum, spent six hours virtually dismantling the space and checking conformance to the lease and building codes. For his final act, he produced from his bag of tricks a device called a *sling psychrometer:* basically two thermometers on the end of a three-foot sling, showing matching temperatures. He placed a wet cloth over one thermometer and swung the device around his head for one minute like a porcine David taking a bead on Goliath. At the end of the minute, the evaporative effect had cooled the wet bulb's reading below that on the dry bulb, and that, property managers, clarifies the wet-bulb language in our leases. We've encountered it in practice once in 24 years, and you'll probably hear "sling psychrometer" on *Jeopardy!* sooner than you will around your office. (And State Farm spent five years in our building, so we must have passed.)

Emergency Escape Routes

There's no need to use a lot of ink on this topic, because the escape maps tend to vary by locale and are frequently dictated by a protocol from the local fire department.

In basic terms, the routes are posted in prominent locations by elevator lobbies and fire exits and stairwells, under a protective cover with a "You Are Here" legend and a series of colored lines to indicate safe primary and alternate routes to a safe area of the floor, then to the exterior of the building.

Good sense dictated these many years before they became required, together with periodic reinforcement of the plan with the building occupants.

*   *   *   *

It was a toss-up whether to include this short note in the *building,* the *visuals,* or the *liaison* chapter. Keep exiting maps in the back of your mind as you read the later chapters "Signs and Visuals" and "Liaison."

Halftime

We'll take a breather here, but stay within the building for a few more chapters before we go out and look around the grounds.

Thus far we've had a look at the physical plant from the management standpoint: the elevators, illumination and heating. In the chapter to come, more hardware—not, as we said, to turn us all into building contractors and architects, but enough to instill a sound knowledge of the physical plants we manage.

We'll meet back in the lobby after this break and continue the tour.

3

The Building, Part II

Our home state's principal economic livelihood occurs in structures that would send cold chills up most property managers' spines: buildings with no doors to close after hours, no drinking fountains or clocks on the walls, few if any exterior windows and attics high enough for employees to sit and watch customers below through one-way glass in the ceiling.

But the granddaddy of them all, Harold's Club, set the pace in the late 1940s. (We'll talk later of on-premises power generation and fuel storage.) Harold's had a two-story Fairbanks-Morse diesel generator from a World War II submarine to keep the lights burning when the power went out and buried a railroad tank car under Virginia Street to keep fuel at the ready.

We predicted roof damage from a TV dish a chapter ago—ponder now the Harold's naval winch, bolted to the roof, to raise and lower a blimp moored a hundred feet above town, "Harold's Club or Bust" on the fuselage welcomed visitors arriving over Donner Pass from California. Now that's roof stress!

(And every Monday morning, blocks from casino row, the author, as a schoolboy, would feel vibration on the classroom floor while the generator was tested.)

*   *   *   *

We reconvene in the lobby of our office building for a walking tour and highlights of some points of interest along the way.

Now we will focus on utilities: gas, power and water distribution; metering and emergency management; telephone and data installations; roof access; subfloor power; phone and data ducting and finally on-site power generation. We reiterate that we're touring an office building, but many parallels exist in the retail centers we also manage. The first item on the agenda is proof positive of that parallel—look in an accessible open area behind the center or office building for:

Utility Services and Cabinets

Leading off with electrical power, we'll state this early: Find out what types of power are available to your building when you assume the management. Your local utility supplier can help you; the usual forms are *single* phase (rare in commercial buildings), *split* phase, *three* phase and a weird breed known as *delta* phase, prevalent in industrial applications, rare in the little buildings we're reading about here. (We're making the assumption that your building has 208-volt or 220-volt service, not the more exotic 440-volt industrial variety.)

You will reap the benefit of this knowledge primarily during the leasing function, when a prospective tenant may ask if one of these choices is available for some electrical appliance they anticipate installing. Don't enroll in engineering school to understand the nuances, just know that *phase* differences exist and acquire sufficient knowledge to give a prospect hope for an informed answer after a call to the utility company.

Meters and Breakers.   At some location in every building across the land there is a location where two things happen: (1) utility services such as electricity, natural gas and water (leave the control and ownership of the utility supplier and entering the control thereafter (or "downstream") of the utility customer. (2) the amount of delivered service is measured, so that the customer may be billed. A primary purchaser (in effect, a lessor acting as a wholesaler), may under some conditions resell energy to a later user (the tenant).

In the proximity of the electrical cabinet we find groups of meters and circuit breakers. While some equipment may exist in the electrical cabinet or distribution area "upstream" of the meter, that area is sealed, as the domain of the power company for testing and internal control, and stringent measures indeed would be taken if the seals were to be broken.

The meters themselves are not particularly noteworthy from the property-management standpoint, since we don't administer them directly. The simplest are the good old glass jars over four or five mechanical pointers, reading out units, tens, hundreds and so on, of kilowatt-hours—just like the meter at home. In some situations the meter may be armored by a sheet-metal cover to prevent vandalism, and in other locales analog pointers are being replaced by digital LCD readouts.

The "Demand" Meter.   Up one level from the basic meter is a recording type that not only reads kilowatt hours, but has a supplemental dial that's zeroed after each meter reading. Venturing an explanation threatens technical gibberish we'd sooner avoid, but in simplest terms, this meter is used to record usage for a billing schedule available to larger electrical users that encourages spreading power consumption over more of the hours in a day and the days of the week. The supplemental dial "samples" power consumption periodically, say every 15 minutes, and records the intervals where power use was high. Thus, a building owner using 30,000 kilowatt-hours over a nine-hour period, Monday through Friday, would pay more per KWH than the user who spread the same consumption over a twelve-hour period six days a week.

In our town, a property-management firm assumed control of a ten-month-old, 46,000-square-foot building in 1982, and a sharp agent noticed the absence of the "recording" meter on the building's master panel. The firm succeeded in imputing the utility vendor's lowest conceivable saving under their large-user tariff. The recomputation resulted in a refund to the building owners in excess of $3,000, which they considered as incidental building income and commissionable to the management firm in the same fashion as rent. Not a bad day's work!

Circuit Breakers.   Somewhere within the mechanical room of the building or in a weatherproof cabinet outside, you're likely to find a bank or two of circuit breakers, big ones, ones that you don't want to turn off just to change a light fixture.

In the typical modern building these are the main breakers, each feeding a smaller cabinet somewhere in the building. In many installations, each breaker feeds one tenancy or some other geographic or generic area of a building, e.g., the subfloor power ducting versus the overhead lighting, or the rooftop HVAC units.

Closer to these areas is a smaller cabinet (often called a *load center*), enclosing breakers of the size we see in our homes. *These* are the ones we can shut off to work on individual circuits!

Several thoughts here: The Uniform Electrical Code requires that all breakers be marked for the circuits that they control; most locales won't allow a breaker panel to be placed behind the swing area of a door; each individual main breaker feeding a load center may, or may not, have its own meter.

We'll also learn in a later chapter how the fire department can turn off a circuit (or "open" it, in the parlance of Reddy Kilowatt), with a *shunt trip breaker* before entering a building.

Locking Cabinets.   In many areas it makes good sense to lock exterior electrical cabinets to prevent unauthorized tampering, which may range from inquisitive teenagers to informed perpetrators creating darkness with malice aforethought. And the typical raintight cabinet has a hasp for a padlock.

But: If we put our lock on, the utility company can't read the meter(s) within, or do necessary maintenance work on the equipment. But if they put their "company" lock on them, then we're on the outside looking in if *we* need access. A suggestion here, with a rough drawing accompanying in figure 1, is a bar or strap, with a hole on either end for a padlock, so that we may lock one end and the power company lock the other, and either party can slide the bar or strap off the hasp for access.

These contraptions, easy to fabricate, are also slick for dumpster enclosures, gates and a variety of other locations where a padlock is desirable but two entities need access. In some instances we just all share keys, but some firms, like trash removal and utility companies, aren't about to give us their master padlock key.

Natural Gas and Water Meters.   The state of the art for all forms of meters (including power) is remote reading capability, where a meter can be "read" at a dial distant from the measuring device. These are valuable from our standpoint as managers, because they may enable us to lock or secure the area where the meter is physically located.

Figure 1. Equal-Access Locking for the Utility Cabinet.

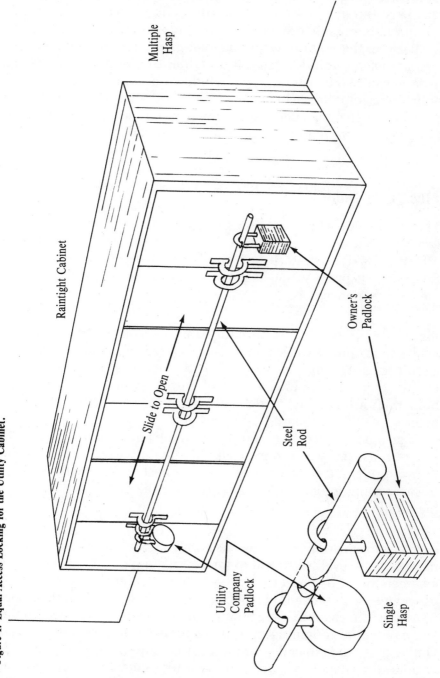

Multiple Hasp

Raintight Cabinet

Slide to Open

Steel Rod

Owner's Padlock

Utility Company Padlock

Single Hasp

(And we're told the time is near when meters may be interrogated by telemetry, infrared or some other medium from a service vehicle passing through a neighborhood or even from an aircraft.)

Back on the ground, we'll note that gas meters, unlike power meters, are usually not located within a building or confined area and usually can't be located under a window—a point of interest, but of only minor importance to management. We do have some responsibility to ensure that the meters and above-ground plumbing are protected from vehicle traffic in conformance to local code.

Emergency Shutoffs

This can remain a brief topic, and of some interest is what's an "emergency" for one may to another be only "somebody-wants-to-turn-off-a-utility-for-whatever's-a-good-reason-in-their-own-mind." *Emergency is preservation of life or structural safety; anything else is mere convenience.*

Electricity. Electricity is easy; the breakers usually "trip" if an overload occurs, and in water-prone areas a *GFI* (ground-fault interruptor) circuit trips if energy leaves a safe path and poses a shock potential too small to open a breaker but of sufficient amperage to harm a human. (You probably have a GFI circuit in your bathroom, if your home's relatively modern.)

If an emergency occurs and you want the power off, now, throw the closest breaker. Bear in mind that a big main breaker can bite when thrown under considerable load, and it's best to flip smaller breakers in succession, which will eventually open the circuit you suspect as the problem.

Gas. Seldom does a building custodian at the occupant or property-management level have need to turn off natural gas in response to an emergency, but if you must, a valve is located at the gas meter—a pliers or crescent wrench is all you need to turn the valve handle perpendicular to the gas line. Do get help when reopening the valve, unless you're adept at relighting pilot lights on water heaters and furnaces. Our suggestion is to call your local utility supplier—the phrase *odor of natural gas* spoken quietly to the utility company's operator will probably bring a pro to your building quicker than you can arrive there.

Water.   Last in our triune of fugitive utilities is water, the commodity that seldom if ever harmed a hair on a tenant's head, but that causes more problems for building managers than a junior high school being built on the vacant lot across the street. Water is controlled by a valve—a device, property managers suspect, that student architects need to learn how to hide before they receive their BA degree and state certification.

As you embark on a career in management, heed these words, and the price of this book will find its way back to you: Determine where the water service(s) to buildings under your supervision are located, before the need to locate them exists. Mark curb valves, valves in mechanical rooms and valves on individual floors, put attractive, businesslike signs or tags on them and paint the ones under parking lots or landscaping with *blue* spray paint (recognized as a color code for water—gas is *yellow*). Show your tenants, landscaping people, janitors and anyone else who may be around when a water line breaks or freezes how to shut off the water.

If the only way to shut a valve is with a ''deep'' key to a valve below the frost line, buy a key with the head-pattern that fits the valve, mark it so the world will know what it is and keep it in some logical location. (Note—if your building has automatic fire sprinklers, don't disturb the service to the sprinkler risers. More about all that in pages to follow.)

The reader was mercifully spared the author's ferocity while banging the above words into the keyboard of our Royal portable, but like many serious building managers, we're a little intense about water escaping from pipelines. The frequent half-hour Aquacades, lacking only Esther Williams and Shamu, seen around commercial buildings while someone is splashing around looking for a valve, bespeaks bad management, and readers of this book are capable of better. End of author's personal diatribe.

Let's Hear It for Ma Bell

With curmudgeonly nostalgia, we'll recall the hot-and-cold love affair of every building manager of yesteryear with that grand lady, Ma Bell, who maintained in her quarters (the phone room) on his property a piece of plywood to which was bolted a Western Electric KS61 switching box that hummed and clicked and smoked the wall up; as well as a rack of smelly wet-cell batteries for dispatching calls to every nook and cranny of the building if the power went out (and was capable of blowing the place higher than a kite if the hydrogen accumulated in her phone room).

We recall building a smallish office building for an insurance company in 1972. And we remember well the phone equipment: a 12-foot wide, floor-to-ceiling metal cabinet enclosing noisy switching equipment drawing 4,000 watts of power, creating an additional heat load on the air conditioning, and from which cabinet a separate half-inch diameter, ''25-pair'' cable led to each of the hundred phones in the building. The cable group easily filled a 12-inch trough from the equipment cabinet to the floor ducting leading out to the phone sets.

In recent years, this equipment was replaced with a cabinet no bigger than a big microwave oven, with minimal power drain, creating no noise or heat, having higher switching capability and employing residential-scale phone wiring to the sets. The balance of the phone equipment room, some 36 square feet, became available for file storage.

Times have changed, mostly for the better phone-wise, but in our multitenant buildings we do become a link in the chain with the telephone companies, the phone equipment installer and the tenant. In many cases one, two or all three will need access to or facilities in the common area of the building (outside the tenant's demised premises), particularly within the office-building setting—less in retail centers.

Before hanging up on the telephone segment, we will let you in on this little timesaver: shorthand for telephone (location, conduit, outlet, equipment room, etc.) in architectural, mechanical and management circles and on blueprints is a *triangle* △ . Incidentally, for power the symbol is a circle with two vertical lines through it ⏀ for 110 volt, or three lines ⏇ for 220 volt:

Public Telephones.   A public toll telephone location is at once a minor responsibility to a property manager and a revenue-generating nonhuman tenant—occasionally quite a lucrative one. We might have such a set in our office building, but the words here are primarily about retail centers.

The facilities supplied by our principal/owner are a phone conduit and power source, usually from the "common area" or "house" power meter. The typical booth or wall-mounted toll set will be illuminated, unless it's in a location with other dusk-to-dawn lighting.

As managers, we might get a complaint now and then over a ripped-up directory or a mix-up in coin change, but the positive effects of customer or tenant convenience and public safety made available by the 9–1–1 system offset these minor problems. And the $10 or $15 checks that dribble in every month usually take the rest of the sting out of public phone maintenance.

Computer Equipment

While we have long been familiar with power, water and gas lines running through our buildings, in the information age, we must also allow for computer networks. Cable pairs for data processing equipment, once the stepchild of telephone cabling, are integral to the design of every modern office building. And, like telephone equipment, sharp management calls for flexibility and ease in the rerouting of cable pairs to accommodate changes in the tenant's floor plan. Don't be surprised if an architect specifies built-up final floors consisting of two- by four-foot panels resting on a gridwork a foot above the structural floor. In computer-intensive offices, this dead space below the floor allows for ventilation and easy access to computer cable arrays by simply lifting a floor panel.

The Roof Scuttle

In many cities, the building code mandates a *roof scuttle*, particularly when the structure is more than one story high. The device is simple and we've seen only one model of the thing: a sheet metal frame two feet square, bolted to the roof, with a hinged weatherproof lid for a workman to open much as John Wayne threw open the hatch of a submarine and stepped onto the conning tower. In this case our sailor is probably going to service a rooftop air conditioner, but if it makes him feel for a moment like the Duke, more the better.

Required or not, a ladder permanently mounted on a wall inside the building ascending to the roof scuttle is safer than a ladder leaning against the side of a building. Many managers journey to the auto parts store and purchase an automotive flashlight holder and flashlight and mount the light near the scuttle ready for use should the need arise to reset a furnace or some such thing after dark. In similar fashion, we tie a rope to the top rung of the ladder, which is just swell to hoist a toolbox or parts up to the roof after climbing the ladder unencumbered by the load. Confirm periodically that the scuttle lid's closed, as most are located in a storeroom or nonvisible area, and a prolonged time with the lid left open results in a broom closet full of dust and dirt, moisture from snow and rain and evidence of feathered friends stopping by. We know. Our experience led us once to wire a blinking lamp in a prominent area of an office ceiling to a microswitch on the scuttle to alert us to an open scuttle.

And the padlock hasp isn't a bad feature, if your roof seems to draw visitors, originating above or below the roof. We're not only concerned about burglars gaining access: A friend of ours owns a three-story building in town, and accidentally discovered 75 percent of his employees and their families having a Yankee Doodle Dandy of a time on the roof of his building at dusk one July Fourth, awaiting a view of the local fireworks. Many a picnic lunch or all-over suntan have been enjoyed on the upside of a roof scuttle, and at this writing a daredevil pastime called bungee-cord jumping is coming into vogue. Lock the things up—they don't get that much legitimate use.

Walker Subfloor Ducting

Note, if you will, in the next few buildings you enter, a so-called *monument* on the floor of an office, with a power plug, phone outlet or data line plugged into it. This monument sits atop a duct, most frequently referred to as a *Walker* duct, a steel conduit about two inches square that runs the length of the office building beneath the floor. The usual duct has an opening just a hair below the poured concrete, every two feet along its length. An electrician can measure from a known opening and chip away concrete to expose a new hole, then pull a circuit to that location—phone, power or data. Or an *abandon plate* can be placed on the floor where a line is no longer needed.

The duct, as we said, has holes every two feet; parallel ducting runs are spaced at intervals, usually 8 or 12 feet apart under the floor, and laid before the final concrete layer is poured to provide a wide selection of desk spacing by opening or abandoning locations in the duct during the life of the building.

If you take over an older building with no subfloor ducting, you may suggest "trees" to the tenants: lightweight, decorative posts running up to and through a false ceiling to phone, power and data conduits. They're not as slick as subfloor ducts, but they are pleasing to most building inspectors, who won't permit more than a six-foot electrical extension cord in a commercial building.

The final observation about subfloor conduit: The text above at first draft was aligned toward an office environment, but progressive retail architects and builders have, in the last decade, provided if not full two-foot variable interval ducting, at least sub-slab conduits to accommodate power outlets where cash registers or phones in retail tenancies are predictable.

On-Site Power

We have the feeling that the reason you've hung around this long in the chapter is to hear how the two-story Fairbanks-Morse diesel mentioned in the opening paragraphs of this chapter cranked up and turned a six-foot armature on the generator to light our little office building and throb under your feet, but you're in for a disappointment. For most of us managing properties of the size we address in this book, we'll have only a handful of candles or a quiet little putt-putt Onan or Kohler generator, only a notch bigger than one in a Winnebago motor home. That's all we need for standby power to a limited number of necessities in a smallish office building.

Of major importance in a power outage is life safety, and we'll find battery-pack-supported emergency lights mandated in key areas of our buildings to illuminate the stairwells and dark areas. Similarly, most alarm equipment is supported by batteries, being constantly charged while off-premises power is available.

Computers and Power.   The toughies to accommodate are the computer users in the building, who can lose significant data even during an outage measurable in milliseconds. On-premises power generation in a typical office building cannot engage in anywhere near this interval. Most serious data users employ a battery system capable of shunting sufficient power to data processing equipment in *nanoseconds* when an outage occurs, thus preserving the unstored data. Their data equipment suppliers usually install and service this standby equipment, and it is not a concern of property management.

Small, down-home property managers of buildings with data equipment can do their tenants a favor by pointing out that most power failures (save for the ones that occur three states away and take out the whole regional power grid!) are predictable, and during lightning storms or periods of peak air conditioning use, power may fluctuate, "bump" or fail completely. Those are good times to shut down the computers until the threat of a failure passes.

*   *   *   *

So, as managers, you'll find only a limited need for stronger short-term power or standby power over a longer duration than batteries can provide. One application that has a greater need is refrigeration equipment, another is electronic data or radio transmission backup. The no-nonsense users are those dependent on medical equipment, such as respirators or dialysis machines. (Medical professionals well acquainted with alternate power sources usually become involved with these applications.) And, as stated in an earlier chapter, some on-premises power facilities may be connected to elevator relays, critical cash-handling areas and other security functions.

As property managers, we're seldom involved at the outset in identifying need for on-premises generation. There's plenty of architects, building owners, tenants, insurance companies and medical people to spell out the desire or true need. What we do is understand how the things work, and keep them working—frequently, the devices will sit unnoticed for months or a year unless someone comes along and tests them, and that someone is usually us.

In most cases, well-designed on-premises power units react to cessation of off-premises (utility) power. A diode (the brains of the outfit) senses that no power is coming over the wires from the usual source, then waits for an interval before activating the system (to make sure that the loss of power isn't just a momentary "bump"). If the power stays off (or low) for more than a few seconds, the generator's control takes several actions (and here, we might oversimplify a bit to keep the text in a layman's purview).

The first automatic activity is to get the generator producing power. The system, like a driver turning the key to a car, starts the generator engine running, drawing power from batteries that have been continuously charging while the power is on (and that the property manager has checked periodically). As the engine builds up speed, the system "brain" samples the power output available from the generator. Remember, a few seconds, or maybe a minute, has elapsed since the lights first went out. This is no "instantaneous" process.

Somewhere about now, the brain samples the power, if any, available from the utility—it might have been restored, and we don't want juice coming from two directions. If it's still off, the brain isolates the electrical system of the building into critical and nonessential zones by opening a shunt (a sort of electrical valve), and the power—now being generated on premises—flows through to the medical equipment, the elevators, the security area or wherever power is critically needed.

Minor Notes: This event will trigger an alarm alerting the property manager that the generator has started. Back at the property, the brain will detect the restoration of off-premises power when that occurs and monitor the incoming voltage. When it is up to snuff, the brain will disconnect the generation system and reshunt purchased power back to the building.

Be aware of a fireman's nightmare: Cutting the normal outside building power with the shunt trip breaker, but allowing (or causing!) the internal generator to continue to send power through some of the circuits. Rest assured that the fire and building inspectors in your town will show you how to properly wire your building to avoid this eventuality.

In a similar vein, we cooperate with the local power company in ensuring that our generated power will not feed back into the line and injure a utility worker. We'll not techspeak here, but offer the peril as information to be aware of when working with building owners and contractors.

Why is this in a property manager's textbook? we heard a reader ask—*this is the stuff of electrical engineers, architects, medical people, the fire department, tenants and building inspectors.* A valid question, but the equipment, if not for us to design or install, is usually ours to test periodically, by mimicking a power failure and waiting for the rumble of a generator engine to start automatically. Our secondary concern with the system is to preserve a supply of fuel for the engine (which is usually propane on the smaller units, diesel for heavier uses). The further questions posed by such fuel storage, in or around an office building or shopping center, we'll leave to officials in your own geographical area.

*   *   *   *

We've a pocketful of notes left over about other components of the physical plant aspect of management, but we're going to include the stuff of those notes under their own headings: sprinklers, alarms, and signs and visuals. Some topics are more about the outside of a building than the inside, so they'll be treated in among our concerns with parking lots.

Night has fallen over our building since we began this tour, so we'll walk outside with a flashlight and resurrect an aging yarn to lead off a chapter about alarms.

4

Alarms

The charcoal-black plume curling above the building was nearly imperceptible against the dark sky, but the beam from our flashlight traced the column of smoke down to its source in the squirrel cage of a pre-Coolidge ventilator.

This was years before 9-1-1, so we dialed the fire department longhand: "I'm reporting an electrical fire in a single-story building, no threat to life safety, no dangerous or explosive materials present." Firefighters like all the information they can get, early.

"Roger, rolling," said the dispatcher. "Wait—how do we get there?"

"Don't you still drive the big red trucks...?"

*   *   *   *

Two early revelations about fire arrived into our life in a virtual dead heat, somewhere around the second grade. As a Tenderfoot member of Cub Scout Pack 304, after having whacked two flint rods against each other a hundred times and then blown tinder all over the scoutmaster's basement to fan a spark that never glowed, we learned that fire was almost impossible to create.

Contemporaneously, a friend of dad's filed to run for justice of the peace and sent to school a shoebox full of plastic magnifying glasses with his name and campaign pitch imprinted on the handles.

The fact that Mr. Beemer was an insurance agent is possibly of interest, inasmuch as it took one among us kids only about three hours to start a fire in a sofa while trying to immolate an ant with a magnifying glass. While we'd like to report that the sofa belonged to one of Mr. Beemer's clients, the intervening four decades have clouded our recollection. We do know that he won the election and remained our county J.P./Marryin' Sam for thirty-five years, campaigning every four years thereafter with imprinted flint rods.

The chapter at hand is of alarms—devices to call someone's attention to a remote occurrence. We'll read of automatic and manual alarms, devices to interpret heat or unauthorized entry, sending the information over telephone lines or telegraph circuits. Some systems are old and low-tech; others are state-of-the-art, but all are in the usual retinue of a building manager.

The Hostile Fire

We recognize in insurance terminology and, therefore, within the context of property management, two types of fire: friendly and hostile. Nothing magic here—the "friendlies" are those burning where we want them, that we go out of our way to create: the burners of a furnace or a water heater, for example. The "hostile" are those where they don't belong: in a building or appurtenant structures (e.g., outdoor signs and pumphouses), or in personal property around our buildings, like dumpsters or automobiles. And, as in life, the friendly occasionally become the hostile.

*   *   *   *

We've elected to use this chapter to provide a nontechnical insight into current methods of obligating this hostile visitor to make its presence known, and the facilities used to transmit a warning to the firehouse. The following companion chapter will continue into a layman's look at the automatic technique to extinguish that fire—a sprinkler system.

We write primarily of warning systems common to the structures that most of us may be called upon to manage for an owner/principal. We'll leave the intricate systems like the Towering Inferno's to Paul Newman and the mechanical engineers who design and operate them. As managers, we usually don't delve too deeply into this sophisticated equipment personally—what we're striving for in this text is the ability to carry on an intelligent conversation with a technician when we need their help.

The Local Pull Station

For openers, a brief mention of one of the oldest types of systems we're likely to encounter: the pull box, or pull station. It's usually a red box on the wall either with a button that, when pushed, breaks a glass panel (probably cutting your finger) or with a safer handle that breaks a glass rod as it's pulled. The usual function of these boxes is twofold: They sound an alarm on the premises, alerting all within earshot that a fire has started, and in most cases they light a lamp on a "locator" panel on a prominent wall outside the building, indicating to arriving firefighters the location of the "tripped" station.

One potential shortcoming of the pullbox is that historically people pull the handle appropriately in response to an apparent fire, then upon hearing the alarm assume that the fire department is notified and en route. A critical element on a local station (*local*, as opposed to *reporting*, when the box is tied to a fire station) is a sign in the proximity of the station indicating that THIS HANDLE DOES NOT SUMMON FIRE DEPARTMENT.

Throughout the chapter, we'll echo the thought that now follows: As building managers, our responsibility may include performing required tests on the components—the horn, the batteries if so equipped and the outside locator panel (and all the other equipment we'll write about soon), then noting and logging the results. Or, in other jurisdictions, our responsibility may be only to call licensed technicians who must perform the same tests. We should have spare glass plates or rods available and the key to reset the system and turn out the light in the outside locator.

Another duty is evident: We advise building occupants of scheduled alarm tests. The tenant mix in many buildings permits the alarm to be sounded during working hours. Other tenancies, say medical-dental offices, discourage the Klaxon being set off until after business hours.

And bear in mind that some of these modern bells and whistles also call the elevators to the ground floor and park them there—coop up the CEO in the Otis for ten minutes and you may see smoke you haven't bargained for.

*   *   *   *

All in all, the pull station's a dandy beginning to an alarm system, but it's got a few drawbacks—it's a traditional target for irresponsible adults and inquiring teenagers, virtually guaranteeing an annual false alarm or two. And potentially worse than a false alarm is no alarm when one *should* sound. A human is a requisite part of the system. But lacking a human to pull the handle, we have just the ticket.

Sensors

In virtually all the tenancies and types of buildings that we may have opportunities to manage, we'll probably encounter some level of fire/heat/smoke/motion sensor system. In buildings of modern design they're a passable alternative to the granddaddy of systems that we'll address in the next chapter—sprinklers. In older buildings, built prior to requirements for protection or warning, retrofitted sensor installation (even if in conduit) is somewhat practical, while a mandate for retrofitted fire sprinklers would probably spell economic doom for the building.

In our town, with a probable variation in yours, we have an architecturally magnificent hotel standing vacant these last five years due to stringent Nevada hotel sprinkler requirements enacted after the disastrous 1980 MGM Grand Hotel fire in Las Vegas. The lonely queen of the Truckee River in Reno will probably feel the wrecker's ball soon—a casualty of the technology of misfortune.

We as managers don't need to know a lot about the little sensor buttons on the walls and ceilings of our buildings, other than to tell our tenants not to hang mistletoe or Halloween spiders from them. As a matter of interest, most of them detect not heat but products of combustion: traditional smoke and suspended particulates, as well as a few gasses and other stuff we can't see or sniff. Some do sense heat above a certain temperature; others react to *rate of rise:* they'd be content with a building taking all afternoon to get up to 95° on a hot day, but sound the alarm if the same room rose from 68° to 78° in a short period of time—a few minutes. (We thought these were reserved for specialized or industrial environments until we assumed management of a mobile home park, where the installer had put such a sensor in a sauna in the clubhouse!)

Thinking of the sensor system in the terms of the local pull-station alarm, we now have a reliable hand, not the hand of the inquisitive teenager or inebriated conventioneer, pulling the switch. The logical progression beyond both is toward a "reporting" system—a device that sounds an audible alarm, alerting tenants or guests, and takes the next action: automatic notification to the fire department (or more in tune with most municipalities: notification to an approved alarm contractor with a hotline to the firehouse). As indicated in a fleeting reference above, the system captures the elevators in multiple-story buildings and returns them to the entry floor. Thereafter, until the alarm is reset, only the firefighters, using their own key, can operate the elevator cars.

The Telephone Link

The link to help is usually telephonic. In lightweight systems, prevalent in smaller buildings with limited probability of fire, the alarm "brain" has a dialer programmed to call the alarm contractor or firehouse and transmit a coded notice of the fire. This call is made over the tenant's existing phone—if the line is already in use, the system "captures" the line and places the call.

A more comprehensive system, courting greater approval from the building owner's fire insurance carrier, employs a "dedicated" phone line, reserved for the exclusive use of the alarm system. The advantage? The alarm contractor's computer constantly interrogates the building's transmitter to ensure the continuity of the phone line. If a line failure occurs, by accident or in contemplation of arson, fire and building personnel will be notified so they may heighten security of the building until protection is restored.

The McCullogh Wheel

A final variation of the notification hardware you're likely to encounter is the *McCullogh wheel*, a device that's been around since the first fire-alarm box went on a city street around the turn of the century. The low-tech but reliable transmitter (sometimes called a *Potter wheel* or *Potter loop* after its inventor) is still used today: a perforated, spring-driven wheel revolves and taps out a coded dot-dash message similar to Morse code over a telephone or telegraph line. The receiving party, usually a firehouse, deciphers the code and responds. By its low tech, it attains reliability. No batteries or electronics to fail—just keep the spring wound! You'll encounter these more often in conjunction with automatic sprinklers, the topic of the following chapter.

Minor Notes: Reporting systems are backed up by batteries, and you may have the responsibility to check them. (A dying battery will usually use its last-gasp milliamp of juice to dial the central office and request a replacement.) Most systems have the capability to transmit not only the presence of a fire, but the reporting sensor's location within the building. (This information is valuable to the fire department—a hot first-floor sensor might result in one engine rolling initially, but were it on the third floor they might send a ladder truck with it.)

Most systems also have a manual switch, similar to a pull station, to transmit an alarm when an obvious need exists and a sensor hasn't reacted, or for an exterior fire where no sensors are installed.

Entry and Specialized Alarms

Of obvious interest within the context of these pages is the parallel use of the alarm for entry/burglary/robbery notification. We won't give this a lot of ink, as we've all watched *The Pink Panther* and *Mission: Impossible* and know that weight, body heat, movement or an opening door can sound an alarm, audibly in the building or silently across town. And we've all seen panic buttons in strategic places, to sound a silent alarm. Or sometimes a portable button, looking for all the world like a garage-door opener, to send the panic code.

We'll not elaborate too much about one feature of modern fire/ entry alarms in this book, as it should stay a surprise to bad guys. Your alarm tech can tell you more about it—the clue is ''code + 1.''

And several pages ago we mentioned that an alarm "captures" the phone line if it's in use when the computer wants to send a message. We'll reveal the reason for that here: During the embryonic days of burglar alarms, the bad guys figured out that they could go to a phone booth at the corner market and dial their target's phone number, ''busying-out'' the telephone and preventing the alarm from sending the code for a break-in. Alarm manufacturers have a few tricks up their sleeves, also, hence the modern capability of the alarm to hang up and redial the phone.

Sensors can be programmed to reveal and transmit an identifiable signal for a myriad of perils: foretelling loss of power to vital machinery, e.g., medical or refrigeration equipment. And a button behind a motel desk might transmit a robbery code, while one in the proximity of a swimming pool would tell the dispatcher to send an ambulance/ E.M.T. unit. The alarm unit can be adapted to recognize virtually any occurrence that creates heat, motion, sound or light.

A final comment is that most alarms incorporate a phone line and therefore a phone bill. If your new account gets a bill for a strange phone number that nobody in the building or the accounts payable desk can recognize, it's probably for a dedicated phone line.

*   *   *   *

The sensors form the early-warning system for fires and other types of perils to the buildings we manage—we'll turn now to snuffing the fires out with an automatic sprinkler system, and tie those sensors and phone-link equipment into the valves and flow detectors in the sprinkler lines. Then we'll "mop up" the fire in these two chapters with some thoughts about our function and responsibility in restoring the systems and letting the occupants back into the building.

But sense no cause for alarm here—the words won't get technical, we're only property managers!

5

Fire Sprinklers

During a skull session preparatory to this chapter, we asked the participants to enumerate characters from history that were heavily affected by fire. The most cerebral from this group were Mrs. O'Leary's cow, Blaze Starr and Bud Light. The less cerebral we'll disregard.

But we knew, upon learning from them that Joan of Arc is alive and medium well, that it was time to move on from italic type to the chapter at hand.

*   *   *   *

It didn't take an awfully long time after the smoke started leaking out of the sofa we ignited with Mr. Beemer's magnifying glass in the last chapter for our peer group to realize that what we really needed pronto was some water. And it pained us to dump a dishpan full of water on the fire, for fear of the damage we'd do to the sofa.

The dilemma we faced at this tender age is the same one that fire insurors faced many years ago with the advent of the first automatic fire sprinklers. That truth is that water will surely do some serious short-term damage to a building and render a considerable segment of the furniture, fixtures and merchandise worthless, but it seldom results in reducing the building to a total wreck. Fire, on the other hand, by creating intense heat for a period of time, can terminate the structural integrity of the building's steel skeleton or mortared joints, not to mention vaporizing wood columns, beams and decking.

In response to this logic, the water sprinkler system, albeit with the havoc it can wreak on a structure, has become *de rigueur* in buildings exceeding a certain size, and/or number of stories, and/or size of basement—and in certain types of tenancies because of the degree of difficulty the structure presents in firefighting with the apparatus available. In sum, if providence dictates a catastrophic loss to property, the insurors will take their chances with water in preference to fire. (And expressed in terms of life safety, few people ever drowned in a sprinklered building, but quite a few have succumbed to smoke or heat.)

*   *   *   *

We reiterate here a thought expressed a chapter ago, that as building managers, we have little need for the technical skills required in maintaining such a system or the hydraulic engineering degree necessary to design it, but we do need a certain level of knowledge to be conversant with the terms we will hear from the system technician, fire inspector and insurance surveyor.

The Sprinkler Head

We'll take a brief look at the denominator of all systems, then branch out into the water-supply lines upstream of that denominator. We're talking now about the sprinkler head, the gadget that sticks out of the ceiling and is all that most tenants or occupants of the building ever see of the system. (And provides them a place to hang the mistletoe after you chase it off the fire sensors.)

Look closely at a head, and you'll notice a pair of arms at a V-angle, held together by an oblong metallic disc, about the size of a penny. That disc is the heart and soul of the whole system—it's actually a *fusible link* that melts almost instantly at a predetermined temperature. The majority of sprinkler links used in buildings that we typically manage look like brass (but aren't), and melt at about 125° F. The two little arms are then free to spread apart, allowing a plug to fly off the end of the water pipe and release a stream of water onto the petals of the brass flower below the head. These divert the stream of water in a cone and the fire, deprived of heat and fed only by a water-soaked fuel source, is drowned.

A Final Note: Our comments here are explanatory only and of little consequence to the building manager; they concern the forms of fusible links. Some systems use glass-fluid plugs, with color-coded fluid to denote pop-off heat. And some metallic fusible links are painted in bright color codes to indicate higher or lower temperature heads for specific protection situations.

Two Sprinkler Systems

Reduced to their simplest terms, we'll encounter two types of sprinkler systems in our client's buildings—*wet pipe* and *dry pipe* (the latter sometimes known as an *air system*). We'll wade into the wet-pipe system first.

Wet-Pipe Systems.   The wet-pipe system is more prevalent inside a heated building with only short runs on building exteriors. In a wet system, the pipes are "charged" with water right up to the sprinkler head, with a head of pressure supplied by the municipal utility company and frequently augmented by a water tank on the building's roof or on an adjoining tower. Such a tank, in addition to providing a standby water supply, vastly increases the water pressure in the building's sprinkler system. The drawbacks are that the water in the tank may freeze, and that the tank represents a massive weight to break loose during an earthquake. A hotel near the San Francisco airport suffered major damage in the 1989 Loma Prieta earthquake, not directly from the quake but from the collapse of a rooftop water tank.

The water in the system within the heated areas of the protected building is usually normal *aqua pura*, the same as what flows from the taps in the building. On the exterior of the building, where protection is afforded to parking areas, covered walkways and porches, the system is treated with antifreeze. "Exposure" sprinklers (aimed to keep the protected building cool in the case of a fire in a closely adjoining building) are also treated with antifreeze. In most areas of the country, even where frost occurs only rarely, an annual inspection by a licensed technician is mandated to assure the integrity of the antifreeze "loops" in the system.

The Dry-Pipe System.   This variant of the sprinkler system is usual for protection of a larger expanse of exterior area—most prevalent, in our kind of property management, in parking garages. Think now in terms of protecting the majority of a system from freezing, as contrasted to antifreezing a relatively short run in a wet-pipe system.

The heads and pipes of a dry-pipe system are similar to those of a wet-pipe installation. The operative differences are an automatic water valve at some heated location upstream in the system preventing flow of water into the unheated pipe, and an air compressor/reservoir maintaining constant high air pressure in the system. Slow leaks in the system are tolerated, but the fusing, or "popping off" of a sprinkler head, as a result of fire results in a rapid loss of air pressure in the system. A sensor, noting the drop in air pressure, opens the water valve and allows water to find its way to the open head, where it leaves the system and suppresses the fire.

Very simple, no?

The Riser Room

Okay, building managers, let's assemble now and traipse down to the sprinkler riser room, probably on the ground floor of the building and accessible from the street, well marked for the fire department and close to the Knox box we learned of in the "Access" chapter.

We see a large, probably six-inch, black pipe rising vertically out of the floor and through the ceiling. On that pipe are a large valve wheel and an electrical sensor. This is the main system, leading to the heads in the building.

We also see a smaller pipe, with another valve handle. This pipe usually opens to a floor drain or out onto a sidewalk, and should be marked TEST.

And we might find a third pipe, smaller, and wyeing off the main pipe, with a another valve and electrical sensor. This is the antifreeze line, usually so marked, feeding the heads protecting the exterior areas of the building.

Finally, look up high on the big, main pipe and you'll find another electrical sensor box with a conduit joining the other electrical runs at the alarm system's brain mounted on the wall.

*   *   *   *

What's the meaning of all this? Simple, if we don't make it complicated; and we won't. Hearken back to the language about a head "popping off" and allowing either water to flow (in a wet system), or air to escape causing a valve to allow water into the pipe (dry system). Following either scenario, water will instantly flow past the electrical sensor on the pipe at the top of the riser.

The Flow Wheel.   Inside this sensor box is a little turbine wheel that the water rotates as it flows past. The rotation actuates an electrical signal to the brain to call the fire department. And we should mention that turning on a fire hose in a hose cabinet in the building usually also sends an alarm. (Parenthetically: Any flow usually also turns on an audible gong outside the building.)

The Tamper Switch.   The large valve wheel on the pipe stops the flow of water to the system when the fire is extinguished. (This paragraph is applicable also to the "antifreeze" system valve and sensor.) The sensor on this valve wheel, detecting closure of the valve, transmits a coded *tamper* signal to the alarm contractor. No water flow is indicated, so no big red trucks arrive, but the building manager will get a call to investigate the valve movement.

There are left in the world a few unscrupulous louts who would throw matches, rub flints together or hold a magnifying glass over an unsuccessful business until it burned to the ground, then seek solace in the tropics on the proceeds of the insurance policy. The "tamper" signal was devised to hold them at bay.

The "Test" Valve.   The most important words to remember from this entire chapter are these: **Warn the Fire Department before opening the test valve!**

The only reliable way to test the little butterfly vanes on the shaft inside the main supply pipe is to let the water flow for a short period of time. We do this by opening the "test" valve, which allows some water to flow past the sensor and dump into a nearby drain or onto the parking lot or sidewalk.

If everything's okay, the brain will dial up the alarm monitor and transmit the code for water flow. The alarm monitor, warned by us to expect the alarm, will confirm the system's operation. Then we call and have the system put back in service.

Several decades ago, a building on the San Francisco Peninsula burned to the ground while an alarm monitor interpreted a flow signal as a test!

The above applies to the wet-pipe systems. Dry pipes are a little more fun, and we hope that you won't play with any system, wet or dry, without a technician present. The dry-pipe test is similar: We shunt the water to a drain, as we don't want to flood the dry-pipe system. Then we open an air valve, simulating a popped head. The air pressure drops in the sprinkler line, the sensor should open the water valve, and flow should occur, as in the dry-pipe test.

*   *   *   *

Glancing around the riser room, we'll probably find the alarm company cabinet, where the wires from the flow and tamper switches terminate. From this cabinet also lead a phone line and a line to 110-volt electrical power. A battery in the alarm cabinet, constantly being charged while power is on, takes over and maintains protection during power outages, in most systems for a week or more if necessary. If your building has a McCullogh wheel, you'll see a big brass gadget on the main pipe with a key on a chain to wind the spring. (The McCullogh wheel occasionally is tested also—ditto on warning the firehouse.)

Also in the riser room is another important cabinet, mandated by the fire codes in most towns: a metal box containing a number of spare sprinkler heads and a wrench to remove the old, popped head and tighten the replacement. The mandate's a good one: When a head pops off, for an actual fire or by accident (which happens), all hell breaks loose as water flows, bells ring, the fire department responds and terminates the water flow and/or the fire and someone starts dealing with the mess.

But we don't want the building unprotected, even for an hour, and if we have a supply of new heads, it's a simple matter to unscrew the old one and replace it, then open the main line valve and notify the alarm contractor that you're back on line. In most systems, reopening the main valve will transmit a "restoral" code.

The Halon® System

You'll encounter a few tenancies that aren't exactly enchanted to have a phalanx of water pipes in their ceilings, one wafer-thin fusible link away from creating an astronomical loss to years of stored data or damage to millions of dollars worth of electronics. Or, to subject their employees, working in an electrically dangerous environment, to contend with a sudden and possibly fatal deluge of water.

One might say that an alternative might be to dispense with fusible link heads in those areas and rely on an accentuated fire watch. But insurors, to grant credit for an automatic sprinklered risk in promulgating the policy premium, want the entirety of that risk protected and won't stand still for gaps in the protection.

So, as a compromise to the interests of both sides, engineers specify a Halon® system in those sensitive areas. Halon is an inert gas, stored in pressure bottles within the room and routed in tubes throughout the protected area. Sensors, upon detecting combustion or heat, open a valve on the storage bottle and the gas almost instantaneously displaces the oxygen in the area, suppressing any fire. An audible warning starts the humans scrambling out of the oxygen-void area, and the alarm transmitter notifies the alarm contractor of the incident in the same fashion as it would a fused water sprinkler head.

Halon® systems are sophisticated, and we as managers will not be called upon to work on them, but it's necessary for us to understand them, not only due to the deviation from our building's fire protection, but in assessing extraordinary costs for such a system should a potential tenant want one installed in their space.

*   *   *   *

We've seen the tip of the iceberg in the preceding words about the automatic sprinkler system, which is all we meant to provide in these pages. We need a working knowledge of them, but we seldom actually perform tests and maintenance—most municipal jurisdictions want all that done by a licensed technician.

We do know enough, however, to conduct a little basic system walk-through with our tenants or building employees. It would be unfortunate indeed to have a head fuse and flood a room for five minutes while the fire department was en route to shut it down, when a layman working late in the building could have located a key by prearrangement and closed the main valve in one-tenth that time. This sort of tenant education is integral to the business that we're in.

Loose Ends

Fire Doors.   Two types of fire doors deserve brief mention. Their existence and location is dictated by the fire code and architecture, but the preservation of their effectiveness falls within the purview of the building manager.

The first type is the heavy fire door hung by rollers on an inclined track, which stays open most of the time, held by our old friend, the fusible link (in this case, a bigger link.) We frequently find this type of door near a boiler or furnace room.

In the case of a fire or excessive heat, the link fuses and allows the door to roll, gravity-powered, down the track and finally slam itself shut. While everyone in the whole building will usually hear the thing when it hits the end of the track, a sensor is provided to warn the alarm company that a heat-related event has occurred.

The second category of fire doors is the hinged type, usually located in the middle of long corridors. The doors are fairly massive and are frequently recessed into the wall—they normally go virtually unnoticed. They're operated by a spring closer, similar to the screen door closer on your home, but with industrial-strength power. An electromagnet holds them open, night and day, until an emergency occurs.

Just as modern elevator cars usually return to the ground floor automatically when a sensor detects heat or water flow, these fire doors will close under similar conditions. It's a simple process: The alarm brain shuts off the power to the magnets, and the doors swing shut, creating a series of firebreaks to confine heat and smoke. When the unsafe condition has abated, power is restored to the magnets and the doors are opened manually until they "stick" and hold open.

We include these doors in the text not because we are directly involved in their design or placement, but because we have the clear duty to ensure that our building tenants don't inadvertently block their line of travel with furniture.

Hose Reels.   These need little explanation: Within a cabinet on most multiple-story buildings, one will find a fire extinguisher and a length of cotton hose. The most important comment about the hose is a warning not to turn it on and direct it into an electrical appliance. More germane to this chapter is the note that in many installations, opening the valve to charge this hose will result in a flow alarm to the system dispatcher.

And Finally: The Shunt Trip Breaker!   Saving the best for last is a nice touch, but in this case it's just a boring little element in building management that ties to emergency procedures: the shunt trip breaker.

This is, in simplest terms, a switch *outside* the building that's provided when the main circuit breakers for electrical power within the building are located inside.

Protocol for firefighters in most areas is that the first apparatus to the scene kills the power to a structure so that water may be safely played on the fire. A shunt trip breaker, usually a button visible behind a glass in a cabinet and prominently marked with a red Scotch-lite™ triangle, enables the arriving firefighters to render the building safe.

Like the fire doors cited above, we don't have a lot to do with the placement or design of the shunts, but we should keep them from being obscured by tenant signage or landscaping.

*   *   *   *

One of our favorite and oft-repeated thoughts while writing about and teaching real estate is that we often convey just enough knowledge to let the recipient go forth and wound himself or herself from an informed perspective, and we've done that again here. With what's been conveyed, we can carry out the goal mentioned several pages ago: intelligent cooperation with the experts with whom we will contract to service and certify our entry and fire-alarm equipment.

And may there never breathe a property manager with soul so dead that he or she doesn't instinctively wonder, just for a moment as walking into a building at night, whether the tenant reprogrammed the four-digit entry code without telling him or her, and if the sudden rumble down the street is a teenager's hot-rod or a patrol car responding to a silent alarm.

6

Common Areas and Facilities

We once taught an adult community college class that could charitably and collectively be described as dim. But leases and retail centers always loomed as bright spots for instructor and student alike during any semester's curriculum, and we looked forward to that segment of the text.

The night arrived to teach the doctrine of common area as it relates to multitenant buildings, and, as is our fashion, we invited students to encapsulate their knee-jerk understanding of the management ramifications of the concept. One student took the lead and revealed that she had visited many shopping centers and thereby learned that the common area is where they have model railroad demonstrations and Jett's Petting Zoo.

A majority of her classmates nodded and chimed in their accord. We knew then that when the night came to teach a prorated escrow closing statement that this group would be in serious trouble.

*   *   *   *

With a light hand on the tiller, we'll set a new course for the text: We've taken a hard look at the building—the pages that follow now address some amenities within the building that we're responsible to administer.

And, as in the "Building I and II" chapters, we're just out strolling, seeing elements of a retail center or office building in no particular sequence and stopping for a longer look at those that catch our eye.

We should note that the "Signs and Visuals" and "Merchant's Association" chapters will supplement elements that we may bypass now. So bear with us—we'll cover them all by the end of the book!

Community Rooms

In the retail center it's a *community room*, in an office building the old standby *conference room*, but by either name, it's a facility that contemporary building developers are quick to incorporate into new buildings: an area available to all tenants in common, to convene a large group of people on an infrequent basis.

The motivation is simple, and valid: Few tenants, office or retail, in our small building need a room in which several dozen people can meet more than a few times a year, but when they do need room, they don't want to go down the street to the Holiday Inn. So we reserve an area for common use, stock it with chairs, tables, a coffee pot, an overhead viewer, a VCR and a monitor, a podium and a dozen other gadgets to help stage a meeting or a conference.

All of which we usually have to keep track of: set up an inventory control, and confirm it after each use.

We also schedule the use of the room, and at this stage the word *continuity* comes to mind: A firm and equitable policy must be determined to prioritize use of the room: by which tenant, for how long, who will clean it up, at the peril of how much deposit and during what hours? Do we need parking lot lights on later in the evening to accommodate the meeting? And will the general public be invited to the room to do business, creating a low-cost adjunct to the tenant's rented space? This type of usage will usually result in a cry of "Foul!" by another tenant.

Nontenant and Public Use.   Many centers make these rooms available to the general public, for a price, and the owner's and building insuror's opinion should be solicited on that score. Bear in mind also that there's a possibility of inadvertently renting the room to an entity in competition with a long-term tenant in the center.

A type of use we encourage is a sort of *pro bono publico* donation of the room to groups doing some good in the community, such as a senior's rummage sale or a CPR class. As long as the seniors aren't selling skateboards and Hulk Hogan isn't giving the chest-compress, it would be pretty hard to have any harm come of this type of use, and the people who visit the building in this spirit of goodwill may return to do business with your tenants.

To make clear our warnings of potential short-term competition to valued long-term tenants, and to sketch the limits of goodwill freebie donations to nonprofit groups, we tell a story of how the two merged into one nonprofit nightmare for us several years ago. We donated an unrented retail bay to a school ski club for a ski-swap. The ski club proceeded to invite major ski, boot, binding and apparel distributors, who came and swapped new equipment and clothing for money, at prices well below those of several merchants in and out of our center. PR-wise, we lost big. The moral is to have a firm handle on donated use of properties and be aware that many of us are being buffaloed by fund-raising not-for-profit groups with devastating effects on our long-term tenants in good standing.

Health and Fitness Rooms

The community-room language above favored the retail center; now we'll give the office building equal time. Most of the newer ones, even the smallish ones we treat in this book, have some area for a shower or two and room for some basic exercise machines.

The utopian room is big enough for three or four machines, a few benches, chairs, a decent scale and a TV/VCR set. The trend leans toward a step or "climber" machine, a rower, a Nordic Track–type skier, a stationary bike, a few wall-weights, a dip bar and maybe a pull-up bar. Posters showing people doing exercises properly and height/weight/age charts are available from the equipment suppliers. Most rooms have copious mirrors, and many healthy types like music tapes to set a cadence for exercising. We'll bring a player; let them bring their own tapes.

Note one similarity in the machines: Short of some activity exceeding the design of the equipment, or someone completely falling off one of the things, it would be extremely difficult to make any appreciable noise with the above equipment, and that factor, fellow building managers, is what we strive for.

When early exercise rooms crept into office buildings, the predominant staple was the four-station weight machine with attendant cables, tracks and weights, which was akin to inviting the Ghost of

Christmas Past to come cavort in the basement of an office building. The modern machinery is more in tune with use in a noise-sensitive environment.

Also, the machines we cited above are safe, if used by normal people with moderate intelligence. We sense that, all disclaimers and hold-harmless agreements aside, we still shoulder some responsibility for the people using the machinery and the room, and we'd sooner not have an injury.

The facilities are usually in the common area, and therefore in the domain of building management. Real-life experience indicates that a cadre of the room's die-hard users tends to manage the place and apportion out times for exclusive use or availability for all, or to set men's versus women's hours of use and maintain and lube the equipment, but we should be prepared to step in periodically and make sure it operates for the good of all.

Our primary responsibility is the protection of our principal/ building owner, and the exposure here is injury. The machinery should be intelligently chosen to suit the makeup of the users and inspected to ensure proper operation. The room as a whole should be clean (janitorial service merits a later chapter of its own—"Labor"), and the people who are entitled to use the room should be well identified by a firm access policy. This is probably not a facility for the family or guests of your tenants' employees.

The Snack Room

The sight of a budding Charles Atlas straining against the graphite arms of the Schwinn Bowflex in the exercise room moves us to jog into the community kitchen and nuke last week's leftover pizza in the microwave. This little room, not to be confused with the larger community room of several pages ago, exists in most office buildings of any size at all, and in some retail centers, albeit occasionally as a hole-in-the-wall partitioned off in the receiving dock.

As part of the common area, it's ours to manage, and our building owner usually provides a small refrigerator, maybe a tabletop two-burner stove, a coffee maker and a microwave oven. Building managers joke that the most consummately ugly dishes and silverware that can be located will probably stay on the premises, mostly intact, for two or three years before we have to replace them. We put a great reliance on the merit system here, and let the tenants and their employees know it: We provide the first appliances and utensils—if they walk away, the owner and the management company won't shepherd them back. The next set comes out of the picnic fund/Super Bowl pool. We find that few of them stray.

Frequently an outside service is invited to place vending machines for hot and cold foods, beverages and snacks—the building owner may participate in the profits to a small degree. Remember, these machines are hooked to the building's power, so some compensation is equitable.

This room is important to our duties in the "Labor" chapter, as food is served and stored here, and we'd like it clean. And we'd like the stove turned off at night.

Off-Premises Businesses

In any modern office building or retail center, there are a number of "Service" tenants hard at work that represent a departure from a traditional, mainstream tenant. Some pay rent, others locate with us rent-free (or for ten dollars a year!), but we're still glad to have them, and in some cases, we actually go out and solicit their presence in our office or center.

We write here of the little unmanned kiosk or drop-box type service center—the earliest of these was a good old mailbox on the corner, to save our tenants a trip downtown. Modernize your thinking now to business practices of the 1990s, like a Federal Express pick-up box or a bank's automatic teller machine (ATM). Most modern buildings, even the smaller ones, anticipate these installations and plan ahead to accommodate them.

The debate can ramble over whether Federal Express or the tenant is the benefactor in FedEx's drop box in an office building or a mall. They're saved the cost of sending a courier around the building, tenant by tenant, to collect packages; the tenant is relieved from waiting around until the courier arrives. With box service in place, the tenants' packages go into the hopper, the courier picks them up together and nobody's the loser. And if a carrier's costs hold the line, that saving might be passed on to the shipper.

The trend in common areas is preplanning or retrodesign to accommodate many such services. Newer buildings in our town have lobby rooms chock full of boxes for Hello Federal, Airborne, Express-Mail, DHL, Purolator et al.; newspaper racks for newspapers from Los Angeles and the San Francisco Bay Area, national and local newspapers, phone booths and a UPS center—and a stamp machine. Some sport a wall plaque with a little yellow cab on it; inside its front door is a direct phone to guess who. (The cab company using that device in Reno claims to have invented it!)

Modern density-office design demands a room reserved for U.S. Postal Service employees, where they can sort mail and place it into standard post boxes in the lobby, saving them from making trips all over multiple-story buildings and enabling building tenants to receive mail at their convenience, seven days a week. (Mail slots in tenant's corridor doors are taboo under most new fire codes.) It's a slick system: The postal patron retains a street address, but the delivery point is the box in the lobby. (Get used to the concept—someday soon all of our residential mail will be delivered to such a box system, located at the end of our street. We'll retain *street addresses* to benefit visiting friends, but receive our mail in *boxes*.)

So if some such entity as one of the myriad above asks for reasonable space in a building, on a wall or in the parking areas, we'll probably give it to them. Think of it: Life becomes simpler for our tenants, some off-premises tenants will actually pay for the location, and in the retail context, the use may result in increased business for our retail tenant, by virtue of increased vehicle trips to our center. Case in point: When we finish typing this chapter tonight, we'll take it to Airborne's dropbox in the Old Town Mall for tomorrow's early bird to Chicago, and then we'll go next door for a TCBY yogurt. (Butterscotch swirl, no peanuts.)

Housekeeping Item: Secure written agreements to isolate your principal/building owner from liability arising out of injury to a member of the public traversing your property to patronize these off-premises businesses. In their own strange way, they're tenants, and a businesslike lease must be kept in effect.

The Great Outdoors

Bearing in mind now that there's a lot of common-area grist left for forthcoming chapters about parking areas and visuals, we'll stroll outside and pick up on a few amenities serving all the tenants in the building that don't fall within the text of those chapters. They're small in size, cost and importance, but they deserve brief mention.

Bike Rack.   We'll lead off with a bike rack—at one time almost unheard of in the proximity of a commercial building. (In the early 1970s a tenant wanted a rack for their cycling employees, and the only vendor who carried them locally wasn't sure if they could sell to anyone but a school district. We convinced them that it was legal for an adult to ride a bike and bought the thing.)

Bikes now proliferate, and that's great. From our standpoint as building managers, we want to accommodate our tenant's employees, and we'll even anchor a rack on the shady north side of the building if we can, but here's the real reason for a bike rack: Lacking a place to secure a bike in an area that's somewhat visible from the building, the cyclist will bring a bike inside the building. (At prices ranging up to a thousand dollars for a good bike, we don't blame them.) And a bike, be it of clunker iron or high-tech alloy, is hard on walls, carpet and furniture, so we don't really want them inside. But provide a good rack with a loop to accept the shackle of a lock, then feel free to demand that bikes stay outside or at home. Don't be surprised to see a rack full of empty locks over the weekend. It's okay—many cyclists taking regular rides keep a lock at both ends of the journey.

Park Benches.   Benches or tables with integrated seats are great PR builders, while adding little load to our responsibilities. We like the enameled steel or aluminum variety in our wintry climate, but redwood or cedar is much more attractive on a well-landscaped campus-type setting. Not too much need be added here—bear in mind that lunch-hour use is prevalent, and set automatic sprinklers accordingly. Keep a trash can handy, equip tables with sunshades if trees and foliage don't filter the sun and provide a comfortable level of light if evening use is probable.

The Parcourse® Fitness System.   We nominate this attractive aggregation of redwood timbers, beams and hardware as the most progressive common-area amenity to proliferate in commercial properties in the past decade. The Parcourse® was developed in San Francisco as a collection of exercise stations (18 in a full set), spaced along a pathway at intervals conducive to invite a stroller to punctuate a walk by doing a different exercise at each station. (Each is different: One may be parallel bars, or resemble a sawhorse, stair steps, a walking beam, an inclined sit-up board and so on around the course.) A weatherproof poster stands at each station, depicting proper use of the "machine" and describing the specific benefit to human physiology. The exercises, designed by the best medical and athletic minds in the nation and periodically updated and reviewed, favor strength and toning, stretching and cardiovascular fitness at the user's own pace and duration—the best half-hour a day that a person can spend.

Originally a linear course of a suggested 1¹/₂- to 2-mile length, the concept has been joined by a Parcourse® "cluster"—exercise stations similar to the linear course, set in a condensed group. Either system speaks volumes of your tenants' concern for their employees by conveying a progressive and wholesome atmosphere, right out on the office lawn!

The "look" of the Parcourse® equipment belies the vast benefit it provides—the stations resemble a jungle gym for big kids (nothing this attractive can be good for you!), and they blend into a landscaped area nicely. From our perspective as managers, the machines, made from heavy redwood timber and rustproof steel with no moving parts, are low- to zero-maintenance. (The original Parcourse®, in use on San Francisco's salt-sprayed Marina Green since 1973, looks as good today as the ones in our dry, high Sierra climate: all just like new.)

If you manage a small office building adjoining a 30' by 30' square of land just waiting to be improved, look into the Parcourse® cluster. The company's easy to find: San Francisco information (area code 415). If you manage a bigger complex on a campus-type setting, or a good-size residential or condo project, go for the full linear course.

We're guilty of a little uncharacteristic and unbridled enthusiasm here, but we're allowed to plug just one product per book and the Parcourse® is it for this one!

*   *   *   *

Winding down the walk around the building exterior, we note two amenities that tenants may appreciate: a *phone booth* and a *public transportation shelter.*

We alluded to the phone booth in an earlier chapter—nothing magic here, just two ³/₄″ EMT conduits for power and telephone line, terminating in a wall or an area for a freestanding pedestal phone. We join the telephone companies in insisting on an open, public location where the booth can be illuminated from dusk to dawn by a lamp in the booth, and booth and occupant reasonably protected from an errant motorist.

There are several parallels between the booth and the shelter. Obviously, the shelter is close to the street and bus service, and designed to stop wind and rain, but not to obscure occupants from the view of passing motorists. Light is nice—quite often the commercially fabricated shelters have a Plexiglas™ or Lexan™ roof, to allow light from a streetlight to illuminate the interior of the shelter. If no streetlight's near, we install our own close to the shelter. The shelters generate some paper and trash, so we place a receptacle near and put the shelter and the receptacle on the list of things for our maintenance crew to service.

These shelters in some areas represent another "quasi-tenant," like the Airborne drop box and the ATM of a few paragraphs ago. Frequently, the advertising firm that places ads on public buses also has a shelter program. They might be awaiting your call to place a shelter on your property, in return for the right to advertise on and inside it. These are usually good trades—your employees get a high-quality shelter and the ad firm does all the placement, maintenance and trash removal.

In the property-management game, we never run out of angles!

The Child-Care Center

Our final offering in this common-area chapter might not be a common-area topic, might not be relevant to the small office or retail buildings we've built this book around and might not even be a concern in some real estate markets. But predicated on trends we've heard of around the country, we feel obligated to include a brief mention of the child-care center as a coming amenity, and an occasional obligation, of the property-management industry.

We're not prone to dissect the social issues of America as they relate to real estate, but we are aware that a growing number of double-income families create the necessity of caring for children during the day, and we're aware that parking, traffic, energy and public-transportation dilemmas exacerbate the need to cut down vehicle trips, period.

We won't hazard a guess how your community handles traffic, child care and orderly growth, but we'll tell of a requirement that our local city council has, twice, laid on developers as a condition to building a large manufacturing plant and a large office building:

A child-care center, on-site, large enough to handle the demographically predictable number of the employees' children, had to be integrated into the construction. Our council slid a little on the "on-site" requirement and let one go in next door to the factory, but in basic terms, mom or dad took the little tykes in the morning and dropped them off right next door to work. The up side is that mom or dad can drop over and visit on a coffee break. Another up side is that the population base of both employers formed the base of a student body, both child-care centers thrived on other surrounding businesses' employees' children and our town as a whole came out quite nicely!

This is not an isolated case; other cities preceded Reno in requiring child care as a condition for rezoning, and more have followed. We're not overworking the topic now—the point has been made. As property-management professionals, we will, if we haven't already, become more sensitive to child-care issues. We probably won't be directly involved in the programs; that's the field of other professionals. But lease to them, accommodate them and be aware of their needs we will, and our industry and society will be the better for it.

*   *   *   *

And with that sermon still ringing in our ears, we'll mosey across the driveway to the parking lot.

7

Parking Lots and Traffic

A local tycoon, a legend in his own mind and the proud owner of a four-story office building built over a two-level garage, went on the warpath about cars without his stickers parked in the garage. His property-management company caught the brunt of it, and vowed to clean up their act.

While this drama was unfolding, his son was wending his way home from college across the Great Divide in his pickup. On his first day home, son took dad's wagon to the ski hill, and dad took son's truck to the office.

Many tow trucks can't hook up to a car in parking garages with low ceilings, but in this case the truck worked just fine, after the alert property manager spotted this wayward jalopy taking up valuable space in the boss's garage.

And the son, after a tough day on the slopes, had to run dad from the building to the tow yard in the Taurus, to bail out the pickup without the parking sticker.

Proving that a large part of any building manager's job is the ability to read minds...

* * * *

We challenge the reader to try to remember how long Wiley Coyote's been trying to conquer the Road Runner, and the most recent time that Wiley ever prevailed. Having contemplated that, you'll see a fair parallel between Wiley and a parking lot owner, and our favorite Chaparral and the American driver: The battle can rage for years with neither a solution nor a life-threatening injury, neither ever wins or loses big and the driver usually has the slight popular edge.

With that opinion in mind, we can leave the imponderables of the world to others and tend to the more serious business at hand, of entreating those who *do* belong on our parking lots with professionalism and a concern for safety.

The Layout of the Lot

We're managers, not draftsmen, and the probability is high that parking lot striping exists at the time we take over an account.

A well-laid-out parking lot doesn't just happen—the width of the aisles, the entry angle of the parking spaces, the width and length of those spaces and the radius of the tightest turn in the lot are all significant factors in the lot. It's important to remember that not all the aisles are planned for automobiles; a few are probably designed for emergency vehicles. In our town a clear area with a 45-foot radius must be provided every 400 feet, so that a fire truck can do a U-turn instead of the more dangerous maneuver of backing up. Most towns have a similar requirement, and our lots are designed in part to accommodate the fire code.

The age of the lot layout is revealing. A typical lot is well designed by an architect, approved by the municipal building department, graded, paved and striped. Every year or so thereafter the lot is restriped and every three or four years it's resealed, but the original striping is never completely obliterated and each restriping follows the old lines.

Is the Layout Obsolete?   A trend emerged in the last 20 years, a period that sounds like forever, but many a 20-year-old site plan for lot striping is still in use. The trend is toward shorter, narrower, more agile cars that can negotiate into or back out of smaller, more sharply angled spaces. In 1970 the norm was a space a foot wider and two feet longer than a comtemporary space, and the entry angle into that early space was shallower, with a two-foot wider aisle between parking rows. This diminished space translates to more parking spaces per square foot of your lot.

Realignment. Two thoughts are concurrently important now. The first is that an older-design lot is probably ripe for restriping, with the dual motivation of providing more parking spaces, or if the present space count is acceptable, then to provide increased area for landscaping, visuals or delivery vehicle parking. The second thought is simple: Don't go it alone—hire an architect and have it done properly. We have several home-grown lot designs in our town, and they stand out like sore thumbs to all who use them.

A baseline we've discovered in our area, which may work in yours, is a quick search of the parking lot site plan for handicapped parking space locators. The building departments of most cities require that these zones be shown on preliminary site plans, and the practice became prevalent nationwide in about the same time frame as our metamorphosis to shorter, narrower cars.

If your lot layout predates this 1975–1980 period, you can probably pick up a few spaces in your lot. Fresh in our mind as we write this: A local building owner recently realigned a 180-space lot with no handicapped zones to 186 contemporary-size spaces plus three handicapped spaces and a 24' by 10' space for short-term (UPS) parking, and generally cleaned up a few tight corners in the old design.

An option used by some designers is a "tiered" parking lot, with *standard* and *compact* areas. Our experience in employee and shopper cooperation with this method has been dismal, save for a few odd little areas around the lot where a "big" car won't fit. "Standard" and "compact" are nebulous adjectives, and being as human and devious as anyone, we've been known to designate our 21-foot-long GMC Suburban as a temporary compact if we're five minutes late, the Sierra wind is icy and our load is ponderous. Pick a generous space size, consistent with practice in your area and your building's typical traffic, and stripe it uniformly.

Handicapped Spaces

We hear of some disparity in thinking around the country about handicapped spaces, particularly in terms of how many are required in relation to floor area or employee density, and of the space size or placement in the parking area.

Several characteristics are probably universal to the 50 states: The first is that police agencies in many areas can tag undesignated cars parked in handicapped spaces with a ticket enforceable in the public court system. This is a boon to many of us, particularly in buildings with a number of handicapped employees. In the place of our usual caterwauling to tenants about parking violations, we just pick up the phone and let the police make the point. Once is usually enough.

Public law enforcement on private lots is rare—the other usual enforcement practice targets fire lane violators.

Locally, our ordinance requires that a sign above hood level be posted to mark the H-zone. The blue wheelchair pictograph on a white field painted on the parking space, blue lines and blue curbs are not enough—we need the sign to enforce violations through ticketing. Our neighboring states recognize this standard, and your state probably does also.

A final suggestion, if you are part of the process of getting spaces designated or relocated, is to bear in mind that adapted vans usually have a wheelchair lift either at the rear or the right side. A user-friendly space is best placed where there is least interference with other traffic at the rear of the van and space on the right permits the 40″ lift to fully extend and lower to ground level. We cite the occupational therapy department of your local hospital as a resource for current information on specific-case van parking solutions.

* * * *

The text continues with space marking, and we'll shade toward the office building spaces, where the next few categories of marking usually occur.

Assigned Parking Spaces

As a general rule, our parking predicaments begin the minute that the ink dries on a lease contract wherein a tenant is granted a specifically marked group of spaces or, God forbid, one person is given one specific space. We're aware of the restriction and the tenant's lesser employees are aware of the preferential spaces for their upper echelon, but other visitors or tenants in the building could give a hoot in hell about a RESERVED sign on private property, and they park there. We then, by virtue of granting a parking space concurrent with the lease, often for additional compensation, are in mini-breach of lease while the intruder occupies the space.

For this dilemma, we offer two solutions—one is cheap, the other expensive but effective. The budget solution is to grant a block of parking spaces for a certain number of cars *in common with other tenants* if parking is not at an absolute premium, and sufficient places usually exist on the lot to satisfy all tenants. The early birds get close to the building, and all those granted the privilege get some reserved space. By doing this, we usually reduce the number of assigned spaces to a very few, usually those powerhouses who execute the lease, paychecks and lease payment. We'll pick up with that thought in the discussion about discretion at the end of the "One-Way Exit" section, and run with it a bit further.

If parking *is* at a premium, due to employee density in your building or incursion from off-premises neighbors, forget the aforementioned honor system. You need a gate.

The Gate Arm

We've all seen them, usually between our car and a parking space. The only usual impediment to installation is getting power to the site of the pedestal, if you're retrofitting a lot. Past that, it's simple—the lessee, if granted 14 spaces, has 14 cards issued to them. (Refer back to the "Access" chapter about magnetic cards that can be invalidated and reissued as necessary.) The 14 employees so honored slide the card through the reader on the pedestal and the arm lifts, stays up for a reasonable time and starts down. Slight resistance will start it back up again, preventing damage to a slowpoke driver's car.

Some building operators set the gates to lift automatically at some hour, like 5 P.M., so cars can exit through the entry gate or service people and evening employees can utilize the lot when more spaces are available. They also benefit from the night lighting and security the lot provides.

Here's a neat wrinkle that some gate systems offer: A slug, offered to preferred or recurrent clients, to allow them to enter the gated lot and park in a "guest" area.

And how about emergency entrance? we heard a reader ask. Simple: The fire truck or ambulance nudges the gate. They're designed as a "breakaway" panel. We keep a few extra arms around and order them in quantity. They get hit, by accident or in frustration, fairly frequently.

The One-Way Exit

Method one, not recommended: card- or slug-operated, or by a button placed driver-window-high, to elevate an exit gate (separate from the entry gate). Problem: At quitting time, a succession of drivers all raise the gate and drive off, then the gate lowers onto the following car and breaks.

Better: A Draconian assembly placed below grade level with spikes hinged to retract for exiting cars, but to remain extended and puncture the tires of a car attempting to enter the lot. From a PR standpoint it's a regrettable option, but we in the property-management community didn't originate humanity's lack of consideration for fellow humans, and if the only way we can ensure parking space for our revenue tenants is to embed spikes in the driveway, we'll do so, and so we have. (They look menacing but pose little danger to pedestrian traffic. Short of a Rickey Henderson second-base slide into one, it would be hard to get hurt by the spikes.)

Illuminate that exit, dusk to dawn, not just during the operational hours of the building. And floodlight a sign on the *street* side of the gate, advising all that "tire damage will result if entry is attempted."

And tell your snowplow driver. We learned of Newton's irresistible force meeting an immovable object one blustery morning, and we also learned that Nothing Runs Like a Deere™ until it plows up a spike barrier.

*   *   *   *

Still within the office context, a cry goes out for discretion in space marking. We still visit buildings with "Mr. Dithers" boldly marked on the bumper block in Mr. D's parking space. We suspect that the manager of that building, or Mr. Dithers, has been living in a vacuum for the last two decades.

There are unhappy souls in the world who may not like an executive, or what the exec's company stands for, who would tamper with a car to drive home a point, no pun intended. Likewise, the same ilk might follow him or her home, or to lunch, for an unwanted confrontation. An obligation of property management is the preservation of our principal's and tenants' confidentiality, and unless a person for whatever reasons wants his or her name marked on a space, the practice should be discouraged.

Bumper Stickers

In a similar vein, note that many buildings issue bumper tags designating a vehicle as authorized to park in the lot. In modern practice, we *don't put the building name on the tag!* A building employee using her own car on a weekend should not be obligated to tell the world that she may receive visitors during the work week at the Airport Plaza. Tag manufacturers have dozens of shapes of tag stock and a palette of colors for a tag number. Thus, your building's system can be unique and easy to spot without divulging the car owner's workplace.

Note: These words should be heeded by the apartment and condominium managers who might read this commercial book.

Another tag option finding popularity: A plastic tag to hang on the inside mirror arm, imprinted with the authorized vehicle's owner's employee number. It may be discretely removed after hours or used on a second car. We're told the origin of this tag system was to address the needs of a number of neighboring co-workers who wished to car-pool to work, but only one neighbor merited a parking space. Ride-sharing is Topic A in metropolitan areas, as well it should be, and taking a permanent sticker off a bumper and facilitating an intelligent division of commuting car usage represents a quantum leap forward. In time, the private sector (our tenants) will benefit by a reduction in demand for parking spaces that still leaves room to attract quality personnel.

Oversized Vehicles

The words of the next few pages are common to retail and office occupancies alike (and, we note, to density residential projects). The thrust of the text is twofold: to enable a manager to anticipate parking problems and deal with tenants on a positive basis; second, to include effective language in the lease to tackle the problem if the Mr. Nice Guy approach doesn't work.

We'll start with a prognosis of what large vehicles do to an otherwise orderly parking lot, then offer a few straightforward phrases to include in a lease to maintain the upper hand over these behemoths.

The oversized vehicles that roll into our lots most often are motorhomes and conventional automobiles towing trailers—travel or camping units or golf-cart, boat or utility trailers. The reasons for being in the lot are diverse, but they usually are related to an employee leaving directly from work to go play.

We hate to be pessimistic, but experience dictates that when they visit at least one of these four occurrences will take place:

1. For sure, the vehicle will take up more than one parking space, which may or not be significant.
2. Most of our lots have a tree or two, a sunshade overhang on the building or a light fixture, and motorhomes were put on earth to break off overhead obstructions.
3. There is the good chance that the 36-foot motorhome, arriving at 7 A.M. sharp, can find a place safely anywhere in the lot. When the employee sneaks out the fire exit at 3 o'clock, however, to steer a course south on the San Diego freeway, he'll probably get no more than three feet in any direction before encountering a car, one vehicle will get crunched—and in a duel between an Audi and a Winnebago, bet on the Winnie.
4. In the retail setting, we relate the age-old merchant's perception that if a shop's line-of-sight view to and from a busy street is blocked for more than one stop-light cycle, the business is surely headed for bankruptcy. Merchants pay for exposure, big cars block that exposure and the property manager will hear about it pronto.

*   *   *   *

We've been wordier than necessary, but the linguistics are to help you offer a few reasons to tenants filling the lot with sheet metal why we just can't tolerate large-vehicle parking. If possible, we can find a back stretch in the lot and invite the driver to park the rig there until departure time.

Short-Term Oversize Parking, Retail Department.   From the *life's too short* files: If you can figure out how to convince the school bus drivers taking a 15-minute coffee break at Flo's Diner to park all eight buses somewhere else; or to persuade the snoozing drivers in the sleeper of the Kenworth tractor just in from a 30-hour run from Denver to move the thing away from the croissant shoppe, please write us care of Dearborn Financial Publishing, Inc. The whole management industry has been awaiting your expertise and diplomacy for 40 years. The base assessment of these dilemmas is that they will go away by themselves in about the same time it will take you to solve them, and with a great deal less stress on your part.

Lease Language for Parking Lots

Back now to challenges that reasonable persons can handle, we'll invent a hypothetical windmill for you to lance at: The guy in a Suburban towing a 24′ Bayliner cruiser on the three-axle trailer parked across three parking places (one a handicapped), who tears up your polite note and tells you he's going to stay put.

An initial observation is that our contract is probably with his employer, not with him, so the employer must bear the brunt of our options, which follow:

6,000 lb. GVW.   In our lease with the employer, we have restricted the use of the parking lot to passenger vehicles and light trucks, which we go on to describe in the lease as being *"under 6,000 pounds GVW"* (gross vehicle weight). This rating is not a guesstimate—it's a measurement stamped by the manufacturer inside the vehicle's driver door. In the last 20 years we've offered to read it to several recalcitrant owners, before or after they unlocked the door. Cars and most pickups fall under the 6,000 pound rating.

Aftermarket Conversions.   The weight rating language in the lease is followed by *"and vehicles not equipped with aftermarket equipment adding height, length or width to the vehicle."* That excludes the pickup with the bubble-top camper, a two-foot rear overhang and another foot over each side (not counting the mirrors!) These units are incapable of fitting in a normal parking space, are high enough to damage landscaping and building elements and don't belong in the lot.

Trailers.   If it weren't for vehicles pulling trailers, we'd get off without a hitch.

The next language to include in the lease, following that italicized above, is, *"nor any vehicle otherwise conforming to the above, connected to any trailer or semitrailer, nor such (semi) trailer when not attached to any powered motor vehicle."*

Analysis: The Suburban with the boat violates the lease, and the employer/lessee is responsible to require the employee to comply with the lease. And he can't unhook the trailer and thereby comply with the lease. The unhooked trailer is verboten. And don't forget the "semi"—most offending trailers are in fact semitrailers and you don't want to get whipped on a technicality.

Our preference, you ask? Rant, rave, threaten and cajole, then go home and forget the theatrics. The thing will probably be gone by closing time anyway, and we don't need lasting animosity with tenants or their employees over temporary matters.

And if it shows up again *next* Friday, tow it. More on that in a few pages.

Vehicles as an Art Form.   Drive down the street in front of most retail centers, and you'll note a number of signs, affixed to vehicles which may or may not be operable, placed near the street to attract attention to a business in the center. Much to our other tenants' and our owner's chagrin, we'll probably never eliminate these signs, but with some foresight we might clean them up and improve the appearance of the center. Our ultimate tool is the lease, by a few clauses we include therein.

Operable Vehicles.   In our town one can purchase, for about a hundred bucks, a retired milk truck, a bread truck or a variety of other veteran slab-sided step vans that have been put out to pasture. For another hundred, the relic can be painted stark white, and for a little more, we suspect for a cheeseburger and a beer, an "artist" will replicate a retail store's name and logo on the truck, using a broom or other precision tool as a paintbrush.

And for a cheeseburger, a beer and a few hundred bucks our attorney can add a clause to our retail leases demanding that vehicles on the premises be *currently licensed and operable, with no flat tires, capable of being started by internal battery capacity and movable by the vehicle's own engine and drive train.* That clause eliminates quite a few of these rolling billboards.

We're happy to see a tenant succeed, and if a clean and functional panel truck or van with an attractive sign parked on the perimeter of the center helps business, more's the better. We restrict signs on operable trucks to *the size limit of a permanent sign in our town not requiring a permit,* which around here is 32 square feet. That's a 4′ by 8′ sign, a generous size to read from a street at urban speeds and distances. And we request that they be moved periodically to avoid the color of permanence.

Hand-in-hand with immobile bread trucks go trailers, with huge sandwich-board ads for the center's deli, parked on the perimeter and drawing animosity from other tenants. The trailer, probably a semitrailer, is already restricted by language offered above, but we usually include a trailer designed only to display advertising on our list of no-no's in the lease, and remove them if they show up.

Abandoned Vehicles.   The point to ponder here is whether a vehicle parked while the owner flies to the coast overnight, or the victim of a dead battery left to be dealt with by daylight, qualifies as "abandoned." We think not. (These words might be best read by the security contractor, whose employees usually check lots during early morning hours.)

We're acquainted with a building owner who sterilizes his parking lot every evening at the stroke of midnight, at the expense of bad publicity—and frequently shelling out the cost of an accidental tow to restore peace in the business family. Most property-management firms and reputable tow companies won't deal with such a tyrant.

Our policy is to leave a car undisturbed the first or second night it's left overnight. We might tape a business card on the driver's window on which we have written "Please call our office." That action alone might get the car moving. And we note it in a log book—date, make, color, plates and this little trick: the position of the valve stems on the driver's side, in relation to a clock. A simple "2–8" notation indicates the front stem at 2 o'clock, the rear at 8 o'clock, revealing whether the car is being moved during the day and replaced in the evening. (Movement would surely alter the position of the stems.)

A night later, a firmer: "This car will be removed at your expense if you don't contact this office." We contact the police, who may be seeking the car as stolen. Look for a car rental agency's bar code or license plate frame—in our tourist town, rental cars occasionally don't make it back to the airport. An envelope or other stationery visible inside may offer a clue to ownership and a phone call might get it removed.

The point of all this is that in the average small building parking lot, most overnight cars take care of themselves in a day or two and disappear. We make a good effort at sleuthing out the others before calling the tow truck. And we keep track of those efforts, just in case we have to defend a tow, as in the building owner's son's pickup in the chapter's opener. Unless an unlicensed 30-year-old car has sat dripping oil onto your handicapped parking place for a few days, a day or two won't make a difference, and we usually learn only later that a tow has resulted in embarrassment when all the facts are revealed.

*   *   *   *

The exceptions to this patient attitude are for the vehicles that don't belong, when known owners refuse to comply with your principal's wishes after reasonable warning. Read here the Class A motorhome or the Suburban with a trailer, after several warnings. These, we tow—as we stated, with a sense of failure. Given a choice, we'd sooner avoid The Call, but we're paid to manage the owner's lot on a businesslike basis.

Methods of Control

The Tow Truck.   The olden days of abusive tow practices are over in most areas, and the tow firms are well regulated and interested in doing a dirty job right. They're the experts in your area to whom we defer for part of this language, but one tenet is almost universal: The privacy of ownership of a parking lot and the owner's intent to tow, and the location or phone access to towed vehicles must be stated on a prominent sign. Absent this sign in several prominent places around your lot, the tow company probably won't respond with a truck.

Responsible tow services like to know that you've conducted a diligent search for the owner of an "abandoned" car before they snatch it. Lot owners with abusive tow policies eventually run out of tow services to carry out these heartless towings.

We maintain a good relationship with our favorite tow service, and when the level of cooperation from a tenant plumbs new depths, we can get a tow truck hooked up to an offending motorhome in a trice if the driver ignores our initial requests for compliance. We're sorry if it comes to that, but the ensuing grapevine chatter thus generated guarantees that light-vehicle parking lots will remain exactly that.

The Denver Boot.   This device to immobilize a car was first used in Denver, Colorado, the city that gave us two Johns (Denver and Elway) and the Denver boot. And the Mile-High local gentry probably wish the ominous distinction associated with the latter had originated elsewhere.

The boot locks over a tire to prevent it from turning and has a metal disk covering the lug nuts to prevent the bootee from removing tire and boot, mounting the spare and driving away.

It was devised for law enforcement, mostly to hogtie cars with a plethora of parking tickets and get the owners down to municipal court so they could talk things over with the judge. It was never designed for private lots.

But private companies bought them and formed "booting" services. Instead of towing a car, they boot it. The obvious fallacy in thought is that a booted car parked in the wrong place in a retail center doesn't leave, but stays parked in the wrong place while the owner hangs around and threatens everyone in sight. Tow victims, in contrast, blow their stacks once and then trundle off elsewhere in search of their wheels.

Our recommendation, based upon limited experience and one firsthand observation of the boot at work and the car owner's response: Leave it for law enforcement people. They carry guns. If a car's blocking something, tow it; don't do something that will just keep it there longer.

Speed Bumps.   A quick statement, swelling to the big finish of a long chapter: If you must use speed bumps, watch your drainage to prevent damming up rain or irrigation water, and keep the things painted a bright traffic color. Bumps are a speed deterrent, but they deter little if they can't be seen. The sound of cars crashing over unseen bumps grates on the nerves of drivers and the tenant closest to the bump. More importantly, we'd hate to accidentally dismount a motorcycle driver who didn't see the bump in time. Lawsuits over these occurrences tend to favor the cyclist.

And speaking of motorcycles, . . .

From Oversized Vehicles to the Motorcycle

Not much verbiage is called for here, either: Except for the big Interstates and Voyagers, four cycles can occupy the space devoted to one car. So get a reading on the number of employees and visitors that typically ride to your parking lot, and zone off one vehicle space for each four cycles. Form an area of concrete bumper curbs to keep cars out, leave a two-foot opening for cycles to get through, put up a MOTORCYCLE PARKING sign and avoid having bikes parked among the cars all over the lot.

And if you find a bunch of postcard-size wood blocks in the area during the summer, leave them there—kickstands on heavy cycles, notoriously Harleys, sink into hot asphalt during the heat of the day and eventually the bike will topple. Motorcycle owners keep such blocks handy in warm weather to set the stand on.

*   *   *   *

Much has been said about a flat patch of asphalt, and for the most part it's valuable information. Many property managers learn that parking-lot management, expressed in terms of time spent and annoyance generated, eclipses management of the building itself. Some of the above pointers may snuff out a few fires before they start. We'll include a bit more information about parking lots in other chapters, on topics closer to the relevant text of those chapters.

On now, to new territory. In the early 1980s we first heard the term *visuals* as an emerging science, so we're honoring it in the title of the next chapter. Years ago, we just called them signs!

8

Signs and Visuals

Readers of our prior books know of our penchant for make-believe name associations like Byars and Sellars, and in this chapter about signs we lust after the possibility of leasing space to three of our area's major regional tenants: Warehouse Markets, Wherehouse Tapes and Records and the Men's Wearhouse.

All we'd be missing in this imaginary mall would be a Wendy's and the dear, late Clara Peller: "Wear's the Beef?"

* * * *

Quite a few pages have been turned since we established the scope of buildings that this book is directed toward, and all too frequently we've written of *a* building, *a* parking lot or *a* sprinkler system. To reiterate: This book is of a small office building, one to four stories, under 50,000 square feet and home to a handful of tenants per floor—or it's a book about a 10- to 12-unit shopping center with a like number of local or regional merchants.

This chapter is not about *a* anything, but about entities coming together to do business in the building. Each tenant has a sign, some signs larger and more prominent than others, and the owners of the building place more signs in the common areas. Some signs are elective and unrestricted, others are dictated by the art department of the tenant's franchise agreement. Some signs are required by a municipal ordinance, others by good sense and some are pictographs having universal interpretation without a printed word. And in increasing numbers, some are in a foreign language we don't speak or read.

We as property managers are well situated to enhance the appearance of the building through attractive visuals, and we're required to exhibit some control over the proportion, size, color, text and public interpretation of visuals placed by our tenants.

For the first time in these pages, the building will cease to be star of this show, and the individual tenants will start to diversify the uniformity of the building. We'll start with a structure devoid of any printed word save the municipal building inspector's signature on the coveted Permit to Occupy, and ink in some ideas.

Let's Hear It for the Retail Sign!

It's said nothing happens till somebody sells something, and the best way to have that happen is to tell people where you are, or what you sell. Shakespearean sets included merchant names, early Matthew Brady daguerreotypes clearly showed signs on period buildings; even Pocahontas had THE BUCK STOPS HERE on her wigwam door. Harold's Club in our town, mentioned in an earlier chapter, offered a small sum of money to anyone who would send them a photo of a barn roof with HAROLD'S CLUB OR BUST! and RENO, NEVADA lettered on it.

By some counts, a thousand roofs all over the world, including one at the South Pole, got the treatment. Although the practice stopped in the early 1950s, the last vestiges of the barn-roof slogan are still visible here and there around the land.

*   *   *   *

Harold Smith was a marketing genius, on a low budget to boot, but the barn roof was somebody else's. People can paint their own barns however they choose, but if they're going to decorate our building, we'd like a little control over it!

In our retail centers (the scene of the next few pages), we reserve the right to approve color renderings of proposed signs. We strive to allow tenants to be creative with their outdoor sign ideas (or mall signs, if we're inside a building). And we actually encourage a few of those less creative to put a little firecracker under a store name or sign artwork, to pep it up. We don't need a center full of boring, forgettable businesses. (Some are a little *too* unforgettable—we'll address that syndrome soon!)

The other horn of this dilemma that we constantly impale ourselves upon is to fit all this natural or enhanced creativity within an area loosely approximating a visual balance with the surrounding tenants' signs. And this balance isn't reached with a tape measure around the perimeter of a sign—much of ''balance'' is influenced by color and type style *(font)* within a perimeter. Thus comes the first tip of the chapter: Don't get tangled up arbitrating sign approvals on your own. Secure the service of a reasonably flexible artist as a semireferee to pass judgment on renderings and suggest cures when a denial is indicated.

The "Can"

Many center architects integrate standard tenant bay signs into the development's plans and renderings. In some jurisdictions, approval of the plan includes approval of the tenant signs, saving a dozen trips to and from the building department as the spaces lease out and signs seek city approval.

You'll hear the term *can* applied to the sheet-metal container, in the shape of the intended sign and deep enough for ''back illumination'' (usually fluorescent tubes). Power conduit from the tenant's circuit-breaker panel to the sign may be done at the time of installation; some owners govern the color of the plastic panels forming the background for the sign, others allow color approval on a case basis from the rendering.

Several other considerations for ''can''-type sign administration by property management are:

- Whether any (licensed) sign installer may provide the plastic insert for the owner-supplied can, or a tenant is required to use the owner's contractor
- Whether the can is to be considered as ''demised'' with the lease in the same form and fashion as interior space, or is chargeable over and above the space rent
- A firm policy that still allows the shape or color of the sign to vary

- The number of signs: If a tenant rents three bays, may they have three cans? Or one wide one?

We knew a landlord who lost a lease with a prospective national tenant because the tenant insisted on a lump at one end of the sign to accommodate the tenant's logo. That degree of inflexibility, on balance, is dumb.

Free-Form Art Work

Absent the sheet-metal can to define the perimeter of a sign, we have to work harder to ensure continuity with free-form signs. Our personal choice runs against the cookie-cutter can signs—we prefer well-designed chunks, parts and pieces put together to form a sign. In many cases complicated shapes are sign installers' nightmares, as various wall penetrations are necessary to provide power to illuminate the various elements, and there are more bulbs to burn out; but overall, some variety gives an attractive look to the center.

We challenged community college students to seek examples of retail chain and franchise logos designed to fit on the facia of a retail mall, usually proportional to 3' high by 15' wide (facia height by bay width). Hint: Note that many descenders (the "tails" on y, q, g, p and j), get tucked up to a level with other letters. The artist that designed Mervyn's signs knew this West Coast store was going into malls. (1980s trend: omission of the possessive apostrophe from retail store names: e.g., Weinstocks, right across the mall from Macy's.)

Name Approval

One of our little side duties as small-property managers is that of a part-time leasing agent, and it's while you're wearing that hat that you'll fall heir to this next trap most of us step into:

The prospective tenants, on the verge of signing a lease, ask if *The Flawed Bod* is amenable to center ownership as the name for their planned aerobics studio. And you reply that that name is just ducky with the ownership. (Ducky is a barometer dictated largely by the vacancy factor in the center.) The tenants, predicated upon your approval of their name, race to order business cards, letterhead, signage, imprinted checks and a dozen other nonreturnable tools of the trade.

Unfortunately, when they go for a business license, a certificate of fictitious name, a corporate charter or a phone book listing, they may be turned down because the name is taken. There may be a Flawed Bod across town—or two states away (by owners who are planning an eventual pilgrimage to our state, and have already registered the name in anticipation of that move; in our rapidly growing state, adjoining California, there are dozens of these "dormant registrations," names held for future use).

The message: When the question is asked, which it will be, it's mandatory to tell the tenants that the name's just fine (or ducky) with us, but that numerous other agencies should be consulted prior to carving the name in stone. Few clever names are new to the world, only to your neighborhood. We thought *Fullcourt Press, Ink.*, dreamed up during a high school basketball game, would be a terribly clever name for a publishing company we started a few years ago. We learned later that we were at least the third user of the name, one in the Midwest and the other in New England.

And If You Don't Like the Name or Artwork. . .   To keep this segment within the realm of reality, we'll skim off the top three percent of humanity that seeks to make an objectionable statement in the Yellow Pages, on a personalized license plate or on a sign in our shopping center. When we, the state or Ma Bell put the brakes on their fun, they wave the First Amendment, illegal restraint of trade doctrines and other misconstrued concepts in our faces and threaten litigation. To deal with these types, we'll keep our recommendation brief: Hand them off to your attorney.

The more prevalent reasons for dragging your managerial feet at their choice of name or logo fall loosely into a few categories: Conflict or confusion with another business's name, an ill-conceived choice of name or art or a suggestive name that might raise an eyebrow or two, but not the collective blood pressure of society to the degree indicated in the preceding paragraph.

We'll digress for a moment, to form a preface for the next few pages: Some may say, where do we get off acting as judge and jury, passing or denying a tenant's signs, artwork and business plan? The answer's simple, and you're paid by the owner to assert this point: Continuity of tenancy builds the success of the center, and a name that invites confusion, or an infringement of a copyright that must be abated or falls flat and forgettable does little to enhance the long-term success of the center. Don't guide with an iron hand, but guide, fairly and with plenty of outside input and counsel.

Name Conflict.   Happily, the process of registering a name with your county's fictitious name bureau will avert most of these conflicts before you have to deal with them. Duplicates can't exist.

But close ties can fall through the cracks—witness the three names in the italicized first paragraph of this chapter. All these names are recorded in Washoe County, Nevada, and might be in your county also. And we don't look only at our own center, we look around the neighborhood. If there's a Fast Foto across the street, we'd discourage a Photo Fast #1 in our center. (Both are active names in our area).

Some leases demanded by larger tenants actually prevent us from allowing use of certain names in our centers. You may anticipate that leases of regional and national majors in larger centers will reserve certain names or phraseology for themselves at a future time. Or without reserving a specific name, they may enjoy the right to approve the use of a name by others in the center. As a property manager taking over an existing center, you'd be well advised to screen the leases you inherit for some of these sleeper clauses that otherwise don't come to light until it's too late.

Another frequent problem arises out of use of a copyrighted tradestyle. Inclusion of Garfield and Odie in your new pet store's artwork, or naming the new golf shop *Arnie's Sand Trap*, will probably bring a battery of attorneys to their grand opening. Bitter battles have been fought over this issue, and the big corporations play rough. Unless your tenant's name is Arnie, steer him toward another name. (And the heavyweights have been known to rattle their swords at an entrepreneur's use of even his or her *own* name!)

Coincidentally, just a day or two before sending this manuscript on to our publisher, we saw a new restaurant in town using the name that, months earlier, we had quite arbitrarily chosen to use in the preceding example: Garfield's. Over the entry of Garfield's, a large feline footprint. Bet that by the time this book is published, Garfield's might have used up all nine lives and wasted a considerable expenditure for signage, advertising and printed menus. The restaurant is in a shopping center—sharp management could have prevented the travail that is sure to come.

Note that these conflicts aren't going to get picked up by the county fictitious name registering process. Fortunately few intelligent sign painters will replicate a well-known copyrighted style that would surely wind up in litigation.

More tenants than we would imagine choose a name or likeness incorporating such a tradestyle, little realizing the consequence. Which is that two months into the tenancy, they cave in to pressure and start over with a new name. Our job is to discourage the use of such tradestyles.

Ill-Conceived Names.   This is the not-seeing-the-forest-for-the-trees problem. We encounter retail tenants who want to name their stores after a family member or an abject Norwegian flatfish. L.L. Bean caught on, but it took L.L. many years—we can't wait that long for K.F. Breckenridge to succeed, and if he tried to use that name in our center with no other verbiage, we'd discourage it.

Certain names are temporary—clever today, gone tomorrow. Or they court recognition with just a narrow audience: Alice's Restaurant. Some names invite confusion. In our town we have an "Ofishal," a great place for a seafood dinner—or is it a fish market, or a place to go to stock our aquariums? Actually it's the last, which accounts for the indifference of the waiters.

If your prospective tenant's name (or artwork, the forgotten topic of these paragraphs) doesn't portray a graphic picture of the business to you, gain a consensus from a few friends. It's tough to tell the tenant the name is a clunker, but better it be done now than later.

A Matter of Taste

As building managers of the 1990s in this favored land, we're confronted with some decisions that put us into a hotbox: On the one hand, we're paid good money to manage a building with professionalism and decorum, by a person who might want to bring his or her visiting mother from Winnetka out to see the building without having to explain the inner meaning of a certain tenant's name or artwork.

On the other hand, now come the tenants who want to incorporate a phrase of questionable taste, a double-entendre or a new usage of a familiar old word in a business name, thereby meriting it prominence on an illuminated sign on your building. To support the use of this phrase, word or whatever, they cite its frequent use on TV shows, by leading-edge newspaper columnists, in occasional quotes of high office-holders and during light beer commercials. They insinuate that you're naught but a narrow-minded poop for discouraging its display on a sign on your principal's building.

The dual and simple facts are that we know right from wrong, and the many shades of gray in between, and secondly that we are agents of a principal, to whom we owe the duty of obedience. If that principal chooses, he or she may "yea" or "nay" on the sign and artwork, and that's the end of it. If they delegate it to you, then steer your own ship, fairly and with an open, informed mind. On this score, short of approving a name or graphics that fall in the blatantly unacceptable range, take some comfort in the fact that modern society didn't hand you an easy choice; you're probably no more wrong than you are correct and you're definitely not responsible for the mores of the times.

The Sign in a Foreign Language.   When we took over management of an eight-unit center in 1968, we probably would have raced to an attorney if we were asked to approve an outdoor sign in a language other than English.

A look around many of our larger cities—and in certain parts of the country, the smaller cities—proves that the wind has changed. Many shopping centers have an exterior sign in some foreign language or typestyle, some in conjunction with English, others with no accompanying English words. (Sign manufacturers, accustomed to using computer-generated type faces, are confronted with manual fabrication of some fonts, as the trade races to adapt existing equipment to create a variety of new type fonts. And some languages defy computerization, due to the multiplicity of characters.)

Most of us are feeling our way along in the new management function of passing judgment on a sign we basically can't read. We offer one suggestion: Request that the prospective tenant provide a rough specimen of the sign art, together with a translation. We then offer the artwork, absent the translation, to others in the tenant's ethnic community. Hopefully, their translations will gibe with the tenant's. Words in most languages, like those in English, have a variety of possible meanings.

We're haunted by the specter of six enraged delegates from the Murmansk chapter of the National Organization for Women riding their yaks into our office and swinging scimitars over their heads, because the new cafe's sign doesn't exactly translate from Cyrillic into "Mom's Deli."

*   *   *   *

All that offers a starting point for shopping center visuals, and we're far from finished yet, but at this point we need to get the co-star of the book, the office building, back into the pages. The next few paragraphs apply equally to both occupancies' visual displays.

Adherence to a Theme

The next time you're in a building or center that has a pleasant "feel" to it, look at the signage. The chances are that there's an underlying continuity to most of the signs in the building, save for each tenant's own sign. (And in an office building even those may conform, unless a regional or national business tenant has their own distinctive style.)

The Font.   We'll highlight a word we've used several times already, so that your sign painter will sense that you didn't just fall off the turnip truck: The word is *font*. A font is a family of the visual variations of one type style, and the family resemblance is evident even when that type face is made bolder, or italicized, compressed, expanded, shadowed or outlined. And fonts have a name—this book is set in Melliza style. An art store or print shop can loan you a book of specimen fonts, displaying type styles and their variations in capital, lowercase and numerals.

We in the property-management business are fortunate indeed that a wide selection of type styles is available in a variety of mediums— precut vinyl letters, press-on sheets, plastic stick-on letters and decal transfers. And all are now available in a variety of sizes, colors and variations such as bold, italic and others. (Several decades ago we could find Helvetica and Times Roman, period. Commercial buildings were all lettered like a freeway offramp or the *New York Times*.)

A Logo and a Color.   After choosing an attractive type font to adopt throughout the property, you might want to design a little gadget to tie in to signage, stationery, vehicles and personnel uniforms; and to make available to tenants in "camera ready" form, for their printed material and advertising. Example: If you're managing Roundhouse Plaza, a steam engine would be a natural.

A final consideration is *color*—wherever possible, repetition of one background color for "light on dark" and a second for "dark on light" is effective and prevents a hodge podge of tones. And if you glean nothing else from this chapter, remember that, architecturally, *glass is "black" as a background color.* Dark or black lettering on glass, save for an unusual contrast or backlighting condition, virtually disappears.

Tenant Cooperation.   In the office context now, we find that most professional tenants look with favor on having their firm name represented in the style adopted by building management. We've never rented to those few like Touche + Ross, who preferred the " + " to an "&" (that's called an *ampersand!*), or Esmark, who shaves off the top of their s, but our experience with most national tenants, unless they have some ungodly affinity for uniform representation of their tradestyle, is that they'll fall in line with a snazzy Eurostyle Bold for corridor door signs when everyone else in the building conforms also.

The Lobby Directory

How difficult can it be to administer a directory fabricated from a black feltboard, with a series of parallel grooves to push the little feet on white letters into? It's a simple chore—we just add the name of each tenant as they move in. Alphabetically, of course.

So, we lease to a real estate writer, and put his company name, *Fullcourt Press, Ink.*, in the "F" row. Alas, no one else knows the firm by that name, so we add *Breckenridge, Karl F.* Later, his partner badgers him into equal status, so up goes *Arthurs, Marva.* Since she uses the premises for another endeavor, we place a separate listing under "S": *Seaside Tutoring,* sublisting, *Arthurs, Marva.* And Breckenridge Realty's broker license has somehow survived all this, so that name goes into the "B" row.

A night phone number might be nice, so somewhere we add *324-1539.* And *licensed real estate broker* to satisfy Nevada licensing requirements. And of course, almost forgotten in all this, a suite number: *203*.

Like Sand on the Seashore.   A lobby directory in a large office building can consume about 40 hours a week of a myopic property manager's time, slipping more tiny letters into the slots. There's a few variables we didn't enumerate above: constantly updating the tenants' newly acquired titles and professional designations, e.g., CLU, GRI or LLD—a lobby directory is an ego trip set in ³/₈-inch type. There are arriving and departing partners and an excellent possibility that a firm's principals will want their own alphabetical listing, separate from the firm's. And most buildings have a directory by *floor* as well as *alphabetically*. Thus everything included under *Fullcourt* will be duplicated under *Second Floor*.

A Directory Policy.   We hate to get so persnickety as to advocate anything so formal as lease language to cover what's included, what's an extra charge and what's taboo in a lobby directory. But even in our smaller buildings a firm policy is desirable, to slow down requests for updating the directory.

What you read above forms a hint of the criteria: A firm name, principals in the firm or signatories of the lease, their professional designations and supplemental language, e.g., "licensed real estate broker." These are lettered in at move-in and are on the house. Additions and deletions *within* the firm and separate firms (Seaside Tutoring, in the example above) are chargeable at a hefty enough rate to make the tenants think twice. Phone numbers are candidates for an across-the-board prohibition, as are contrived names like *(Who loves ya, baby?)*, currently being displayed as a middle name in Reno at this writing.

We're accomplishing several goals: The cost of additions might compensate us for our extra time and cause a tenant to curtail their listings, and thereby not fill the board to capacity.

And the pendulum can swing the other way: Twice, in 20 years, we've encountered low-profile tenants who didn't want a name on the directory—for security reasons. Visitors and delivery people seeking these recluses constantly bothered the other tenants and occasionally our office. If it's confined to once a decade, we can handle it, but we'd prefer known tenants, if only known by a coded name in the directory.

The Readerboard

Some managers *like* to move letters around to change a message, so we'll go from the little white ones in the lobby directory of an office to big plastic ones, probably across the street in the retail center.

This is the readerboard, a back-illuminated white acrylic sign with slots for letters and numbers, placed high enough to be seen by passing traffic. Most have four or five lines for characters and, with judicious use, much information may be placed upon the sign. Two thoughts are interesting:

The Science and the Art.   The first to most people is how we work the letters from the ground, and in most cases we use a suction cup on the end of a pole. We place the letter on the suction cup, drop it into the slot high over our head, and twist the pole, popping the suction and releasing the letter. The art of this game is to anticipate what letters in the existing message can be used in the next message, and relocate them first. The unused letters come down, new letters go up and pop off the pole and a new message exists. Most of us, with a little practice, can do both sides of a board with four or five lines of letters in 20 minutes.

The Message.   Putting up the letters is almost enjoyable, but now the tough question: What tenant gets the use of the board with what message? (Remember, there are two sides to most boards, therefore conceivably two tenants can display at once. Then they can argue about the better "traffic" side!)

Assigning space on the board is partially a function of the merchant's association we'll read more of after the "Lease" chapter. If that body exists, we usually let them dictate the display after they arbitrate among themselves for rotation on the readerboard. If we adminster it ourselves, we strike a fair rotation interval and solicit text from the next tenant due up.

We can use the boards effectively in public service, tying the message to civic functions, safe-driving holidays and the like. We inadvertently created a monster by honoring the high school "Jock of the Week" on the readerboard of a center we managed a few years ago. The Tuesday-morning announcement, by the third Tuesday morning, escalated to a media event in our sleepy state capital and brought free photo coverage to this brand-new center. (Our devious intent. . .)

We picked one athlete a week, and all the kids loved the program. But the parents of the also-rans were irritated, and the program soon turned into a political hot potato. We turned to a "Who shot J.R.?" contest, and the "Jock of the Week" hit the showers.

Have some fun with your readerboards, and give all the tenants and the community a fair shot at using them. They're a great PR builder.

An Electronic Readerboard!   When we die and go to retail managers' heaven, we'll be met at the gate by an angel who will check us out on an *electronic* readerboard. This magical transplant from the end zone of a stadium allows us to sit in our office with a computer or paper-tape-punch keyboard (like an old Telex machine), and make another tenant in our center happy every ten seconds as we key in their ads, separated by the correct time, a public service message, the temperature or—in the case of one board in California's East Bay region—a proposal of matrimony. (An anxious suitor used a readerboard to pop the question to a lass known to commute on the freeway adjoining the board—*successfully. Who says romance is dead?)*

Electronic readers range from the simple to the sublime, from monochrome light blubs to diamond-vision color chips and from fixed to animated messages. In our small buildings, we'll probably deal with the simpler ones, but sign costs are dropping, and soon the higher-tech boards will be up on every corner.

Miscellaneous Thoughts: Continuity and fairness to tenants remain important, even though some of them may participate in the electronic board more often. And boards equipped with correct-time modules should be checked occasionally to verify the displayed time.

Political Signs

Text of this semiannual nuisance carries equal impact for retail and office tenancies: The political campaign sign.

It's been a long chapter, and it needn't be too much longer to convey simply that the political preferences of one tenant may not align with those of another tenant or visitors to the building. We must take the steps to ensure that one tenant's campaign sign doesn't create the impression that the sign speaks for the preference of all the tenants in the center or the office building.

Our job is simple and should remain so: Insert a clause in the lease indicating that visual matter endorsing a candidate in a political race for election, partisan and nonpartisan alike, *shall not be displayed in any location within the demised premises visible from any place within the common area.*

And, if it's in the common area, it's yours to remove. (We'll never cure these breaches—about the time we get a flood of complaints and get good and mad about it, everybody votes, somebody gets elected and we go through it all again two years later!)

Miscellaneous Visuals

Rooftop Identification. This is a little offbeat item we're throwing in near the end of our chapter, typically the stuff of larger buildings in larger towns, but finding its way to our small structures: A number on the roof of your building, assigned by a public-safety agency in your town, visible from a police or medical helicopter.

Technology is improving every year to embed such a number into the roof of the building in a contrasting color, to lead help to the building.

Enough said here—local agencies and your architect can help you with the practice in your town. It's a visual visible to few.

Street Numbers. A forgotten visual, but a business builder for your tenants and a matter of good sense: the street number, or range of numbers within a retail strip, displayed on a contrasting background. Generally, white numbers will appear brighter than dark or brass numbers during the evening when headlights are the primary source of illumination. Your fire department probably monitors street signs periodically—beat them to the punch with an orderly set of numbers in the typestyle used throughout the center.

Stars and Stripes Forever. No chapter of visuals could be complete without reference to the American flag, flown above many office buildings and retail centers. We've seldom had difficulty enlisting a cadre of tenants' employees to hoist the flag in the morning and lower it before dark or in inclement weather. Relatively recent changes in flag etiquette permit it to be flown after dark, as long as it is illuminated; thus, many newer buildings have a photocell lamp directed at the flagpole.

Our primary motivation for including the flag in this chapter is to include this one situation that haunts most of us:

As property managers, we are barraged with requests to honor our tenants' long-time employees, family members and customers, or popular civic, sports or governmental figures, upon their death, by lowering the flag to half-staff. In most cases, all agree that such a tribute seems appropriate, but we should be aware that only two people may authorize a flag to be flown at half-staff. Historically, the president of the United States alone held that power, and later the governors of the several states were also granted the authority, in response to more localized events in the growing nation.

You'll hear requests for such a tribute, but be guided by the position of flags on federal and state buildings—they set the pace for the community.

Except for Memorial Day, when the flag is flown at half-staff until noon, then raised fully until sunset.

9

Building Security

For 30 years, a machinist pushed a wheelbarrow through the factory's employee gate at the end of each workday. And for the same 30 years, a security guard lifted the tarpaulin covering the wheelbarrow, revealing only the machinist's toolbox and his lunch pail, and then waved him through.

Coincidentally, the machinist and the security guard retired from the company during the same month, and both were feted to a retirement dinner. As they admired each other's gold watch, the guard turned to the machinist:

"Now that we're both retired, you can give me a straight answer: Why'd you throw the tarp over the wheelbarrow every night like you were hiding something? What were you up to all those years?"

The machinist smiled and replied, "Very simple. I was stealing wheelbarrows."

* * * *

Security

Security implies many things to many people, and during the drought in the flow of the milk of human kindness so apparent as we write these words, security has become a major concern to tenants and their employees, in both the retail and the office setting.

To establish a baseline for the words in the balance of this chapter, we'd like to announce that we're trying to hold a beachhead against whatever aggressors are usual to the typical American neighborhood shopping centers and office plazas. We're not looking through rose-colored glasses at life, and we recall our tenure managing a strip center where the stuff on the floor of the bar wasn't sawdust, but last night's furniture. Such properties do exist—our firm's managed a few—but we write now of the more tranquil places where we all go to work or shop.

And continuing the baseline, our target security force is less the product of crossbreeding descendants of Rambo, Chuck Norris and Mr. T, than just plain employees with an outgoing personality, a facility for thinking on their feet and a desire to help our properties' shoppers and clients. Their major obligation is to act as the eyes and ears of management and ownership. More of that thought will follow.

Security in Perspective

Within the security and safety universe there are two levels of trained people: The first are the public police—psychologically screened prior to being hired by a police or sheriff's office, given rigorous training in people-managing skills, provided with top-flight equipment and sent out into the community with backup resources.

The second level of security is the on-site security employee, and for the balance of these pages we'll assume that he or she is employed by a security contractor who places people on our sites. These people might have less law-enforcement training, sparser equipment and thinner backup, but it's okay—they have the advantage of knowing our properties and our people better than the public police, and they don't have the need to pursue disagreeable situations to the degree that the police do. Their function is to *call* the police, not to replace them. The property manager, in concert with the security contractor's management, can make the life of the ownership, the tenancy, the public and the security force itself a whole lot happier if that priority is kept in the forefront by all concerned.

Uniformed Security

We'll probably never see all the security agents in the business forsake law-enforcement-style uniforms, nor is that always the better idea. But we do recall reading years ago of a major university campus whose student body was locked in constant combat with the campus police.

The campus cops were students, but dressed like their police counterparts downtown, in dark shirts, trousers, shoes and hats, a brass badge and everything the police had, including a two-foot baton, handcuffs and Mace™ canisters hanging from a tooled leather belt.

And black Ray-Bans.

The most serious confrontation they had faced with their fellow students in seven semesters was one panty-raid that became uglier than most. But the student police remained the target of constant abuse.

The university's board of regents took a big step: They dressed the beleaguered campus police in blazers and slacks during daylight and early evening hours. They were recognizable by their distinctive colors, with a fabric patch in place of the brass badge, and all the belt hardware stayed at home.

The life of the campus police immediately calmed down, the students left them to ticket illegally parked cars, rattle doors and the other mundane activities they were intended to do, and everyone matriculated happily ever after.

We've seen the tactic work in other areas: In Disneyland, the security (most with police backgrounds, the best in the business) wear nonthreatening blazers, or turn-of-the-century Keystone-Cop attire, and many municipal police agencies have adopted recognizable but nontraditional law enforcement uniforms for daylight assignments.

The "Host." You'll come to know that security agencies tend to mimic police forces with an American flag, a company patch, etc., etc., but remember who's paying their salary—we are. We have friends in management around the country who have insisted on a change from traditional security uniforms to slacks and an open-collared shirt with a patch on the pocket lettered "Host" or "Security," or light-colored windbreaker with "Host" on the lapel or the back.

The people wearing these "uniforms" patrol in moderate to upscale centers and office buildings. Management noticed positive results almost immediately.

Final Comment: A more traditional law-enforcement-inspired uniform, in the eyes of most managers, remains the sartorially resplendent choice for later evening hours in most complexes and in properties where the tenancy or the clientele responds more readily to the illusion of authority.

Armament and Ordinance.   One occurrence stands vividly in relief in the memory of this writer, so don't look for a great deal of objectivity in this pistol-packin' segment of the book. But this could happen again in your center or mine, tonight. And it happened only in the past few years, in a town that has a basically competent control of firearm licensing *and* certification of security agencies.

A graveyard-shift security agent was patrolling a complex where firearms neither were authorized by management nor were of any particular utility—just a sleepy little retail center.

But the sleepy quickly enlivened when our security agent heard on his walkie-talkie that a person wearing a Levi jacket had just robbed a convenience store near the center.

Three out of five people in Reno wear Levi jackets when the winter winds blow, and one of them was unfortunate enough to be walking across the street when the security guard saw him (or *her*—we'll never know). He/she kept steppin', while the guard hollered "Halt!" then emptied his revolver into a fleeing neon motel sign across the street (two rounds), thin air (three rounds) and a mailbox.

All we learned from this incident is that one can shoot up a motel sign, a guy in a Levi jacket and probably a writer but never, ever a mailbox. The U.S. Postal Service is touchy about people ventilating them with a Smith and Wesson and exact an endless supply of paperwork from perpetrators of such outrages.

*   *   *   *

So how do we feel about pistols, you say? We know that municipal police and other public law enforcement officers are enjoined even from pulling them out of their holsters, let alone firing them, except in response to a short list of instances. And that officers are limited in the type of pistol and bullets they can fire, to prevent hot lead from penetrating walls a block away or damaging human tissue beyond economical repair.

And we look back over a career of management to determine what could possibly have been at risk in our properties to justify shooting at somebody to save it. And we read of trained public police who occasionally hit an innocent party.

Our opinion should be starting to surface: Sidearms, in response to situations usual to a light commercial property, carried by persons with less than professional training, are probably not a great idea, and in fact could escalate a confrontation that might dwindle and die if the emotional element of a gun weren't present.

Armed security is a definite topic to bring up with your principals and their attorneys, insurance underwriters and local police. Most will probably agree that firearms create more problems than they solve.

Tenants, however, who have less exposure than you and the insurors, *like* armed security. Our text might have been bit longer than necessary on the topic, if not for your need for several good reasons to explain why the building security people aren't armed.

The final character in this cast is the security firm or agent, and their usual response is that no man can walk these halls safely without a pistol. If the police agree, arm your people. But if you lack police endorsement of firearms for your case, then you probably do not need that security firm for the property.

Clubs, Flashlights and Handcuffs.   In the earlier pages we were intentionally detailed, and now we'll be equally brief: Reread all you read above about guns—the insurance aspects, proper training, the antagonistic perception, the slim justification for their use and the tragedy that results when one is used incorrectly. Then plug *these* terms into the text: nightstick (or baton), a five-cell aluminum flashlight the length of a billy club, a spray can of Mace™ or cayenne pepper and a set of handcuffs. We discourage all of them as we do sidearms, for similar reasons.

Particular attention might be given to the handcuffs: Detaining a person until the arrival of sworn police under a citizen's arrest doctrine is fine, but restraining them, e.g., with handcuffs, can escalate a relatively insignificant shoplifting ember into a civil-rights brushfire that burns even hotter in most communities if a minor is involved. The larger brunt of guilt usually boomerangs back to the tenant and center management or ownership, unless these matters are handled within a protocol available from local law enforcement and criminal prosecuting attorneys.

Our words from above echo: Restrict or monitor these security tools and practices very closely.

The Eyes and the Ears

Having dressed our security agent in garb somewhat appropriate for the task and relieved them of the burden of packing a carbine around for the next eight hours, we'll send them out into the fray. (Bear in mind, this chapter somewhat exceeds the small buildings we picked for the book, but we're bending the rules just a bit!)

The first order of business is *continuity*, from shift to shift. We hold a miniversion of the changing of the guard. The guard going off duty tells the relief what might come along that shift that deviates from the standard procedure—a tenant bay under construction or an office staying open late, for instance. This should be done in writing, and for most of us, who use a security contractor, it is a function of that contractor. In the "eyes and ears" definition of security, those instructions, together with a contemporaneous log maintained by the patrol person detailing noteworthy occurrences during a shift, are delivered to us each day.

The "Watchman Station"

No gender preference is intended here—the term in the title has been a standard in the building-security and insurance industry for many decades. (An occasional variation is "watchman-with-clock" coverage.) We've all seen the "station" keys in larger office buildings and department stores, many of us without knowing what they are—a small black box with a hinged lid, mounted about shoulder high on a wall, and inside the box a key on a length of chain. The lid is usually marked DETEX®, the name of the firm that supplies the systems. Each key in the Detex® station boxes around the building is different.

The "watchman" carries a wind-up clock about the size of a videocamera, usually on a shoulder strap. A paper disk rotates inside the clock, marked in hours and minutes on a twenty-four-hour scale.

Building management determines a route for the watchman to follow, which will take him or her all over the building, from floor to floor, to all exterior doors and outside the building. Consideration is given of the time necessary for a person on foot to travel from station to station by neither at a dead run nor during an interval long enough to catch forty winks or fill an inside straight.

The watchman arrives at each station, turns the key in the clock to notch the paper disk by the current time and then walks to the next station. The clock will not accept keys out of the prescribed order, and yes, we occasionally change the route and timing, to frustrate a bad guy trying to fit a devious act between the watchman's trips.

*   *   *   *

It's a good system, old as the hills, and still acceptable to insurance companies. Modern technology has replaced the ten-pound clock with a pocketbook-sized microprocessor, which still requires human transportation from sensor to sensor. This modern "clock" allows more flexibility in route changes, relays an error signal to an errant watchman to facilitate a corrected route or sequence and enables a shift supervisor to integrate short-term or specialized route inspection functions into the watchman's activities. And instead of reading a paper disk, we download the watchman's activities into a reader-display.

We've been amazed, several times, when explaining this device in a classroom, that students miss the point of a clock station, so we'll drive it home here: The clock forces a security agent to cover the total-ity of a building, on some sort of schedule, to accomplish the main purpose of security: to look and to listen.

In your travels around commercial property you'll be asked whether you have a watchman station in use. You probably won't, in modern small properties—alarms and sensors do a great job. But the term's a good one to know.

Video Surveillance

In the smaller properties used for this book, a few TV cameras at en-trances and security-critical locations are probably more effective and a lot more economical in the long run than a human being packing a clock around a building.

We harbor the feeling that a fair number of the cameras we see in office lobbies and stores aren't really hooked to anything but the wall, but we don't know for sure, and that's why they do their job.

The ones that are hooked up usually feed to a central unit, which records from one of the cameras in the building for a few seconds, then cycles automatically to the next camera. In some systems a sound or a change in light level switches the machinery to record that area immediately and ignore the programmed sequence.

The taped history of any period of surveillance may be viewed in two ways: One is real time, by a security agent in the building or down the street in the agency's office, possibly tuning in because a sound-actuated sensor sent a signal that a noise was detected. The remote agent can "dial up" that building and choose the camera closest to the sensor, to confirm or deny a penetration of security.

A second method of viewing, prevalent in our smaller buildings, is to choose equipment that makes a continuous videotape of the images of the various cameras. If we'd like to determine whether a particular vehicle entered our parking lot or what time the disposal service picked up our dumpster, we can scan the tape, find the event and read the date and time on the screen. If nothing happens worth reviewing, we just let the tape run. The usual machinery saves images on a tape for some period of time—a day or a week—then "recycles" the tape.

Video monitoring is cost-effective, and the wall-mounted cameras form an excellent deterrent. The pros in your town to talk to are the people who sell and service them. Together with some of the affordable alarm technology cited in an earlier chapter, videocams are rewriting the book in the property-management profession.

A Benefit to Employees

A forgotten benefactor to a good security system is often the employee of a tenant in our mercantile center or office building. We all tend to see a security agent's responsibility as "host" and information agent to shoppers and clients, or as the protector of the owner's and tenants' property when all have gone home, but we have a third responsibility, and we'll hit it hard here: We have people working in the building, before and after the others come to do business, and they need safe passage to and from the workplace.

A popular function of security is escorting employees from the building to their cars. We know of malls that close at 9:00 P.M. and turn their parking lot lights out at 9:05—woe be to the employees. Employees-only parking lot areas are a good idea—they're concentrated, can be patrolled easily and are well-lit until all have gone home.

A variation of this theme benefits those who arrive *early*, prevalent on the West Coast, where many of us go to work at 5 A.M. to accommodate East Coast counterparts who think the day begins at 8 A.M. EST sharp all over the world, and how could those lazy louts in California be asleep when there's a job to be done!

The familiar face of our security agent, even if he's only sipping his coffee and reading the sports page, is a warm sight in the lobby of an office building at 10 minutes till 5 on a December morn.

A constant annoyance to westerners is that Columbus came from the east. Had he stumbled into San Francisco Bay and colonialization had started there, we could go to work at 8:00 and let Wall Street open at 11:00.

Small-Building Security

We'll start to wend our way back to the limited-security needs of a 30,000-square-foot office building or a 12-bay retail center, and admit that those buildings usually don't need on-site security labor.

A few alternatives exist: a part-time person to keep a little law and order after school while the kids pass through the center on the way home, or in early evening from dusk to midnight in some retail centers to make sure all the doors get locked.

Most security contractors offer a drive-through service, dispatching agents on a random timetable to drive through a center several times a night. Or to inventory cars left on a parking lot, office or retail, in the early morning hours, when all that belong there should long since have gone home.

Some can perform a service that has to be done on the property on a repetitive basis: We used one for many years to lock a gate each evening and then unlock it at dawn. Or to advise us when parking lot lights or other lights are burned out so we can replace them. (Did we mention that all gates, parking lot light standards, doors or anything else on a property that exists in pairs or more should be numbered, to facilitate just this purpose?)

As small-property managers, an association with a reliable around-the-clock security firm is valuable. Give them a set of keys and a few emergency names and numbers, and if somebody gets stuck in an elevator you can call them to get the elevator tech in. Or if it snows while you're deep in slumber, they can start your day with a call to get the snow removal crew out. (That crew is occasionally synonymous with the property manager.)

*   *   *   *

In the early pages, we minimized the effectiveness of khaki-clad personnel in Sam Browne belts patrolling our placid little properties with an Uzi, and we stand by that opinion. But security firms have a service to offer, and if you can resolve your security needs with a crew with personality and dressed in distinctive attire, with a set of keys and a walkie-talkie to summon police or medical help when it's dictated, who help out your tenants' employees and customers and tell you everything that happened in your property in the past 24 hours that's worth hearing about, you've built a team to stick with!

10

Labor

American office workers should pay daily homage to their custodial crew, but not just for cleaning up their building each night. The underlying role of the custodians is to provide a whipping-boy, a foil to accept the blame for every item of personal property that's missing from that office.

Were it not for these custodians, the nameless, unseen people who come to clean the office after hours, we'd have only each other to confront, those that we all work with hand-in-glove, eyeball-to-eyeball, one petty thief to another.

We've employed a man for many a year who we'd trust with anything we own. One night we presented him with a mock invoice for everything our tenants had accused him of lifting during a 30-day period: a calculator; an adding machine; a parka; a 49er hat; innumerable pencils, pens and stationery; enough food to nourish an army and two snow tires from the supply room.

Darryl smiled and told us to take it out of his paycheck, but to credit him for the parka that didn't fit, adjust our overcharge for the hat and to include an Eskimo Pie that they'd missed in the inventory.

Somehow, we knew that the Eskimo Pie was the only booty that had left the building with Darryl.

*   *   *   *

The casual observer might ask how management of a dozen-unit neighborhood retail center or a small office building could possibly require anybody on the payroll on any steady basis.

Those readers would be right, if that's all we managed. But, in the larger scheme of things, this book is targeted toward the people and offices who have two or three small centers and a like number of offices under management. With that degree of responsibility, we all need help to a depth and a number of hours justifying a full-time security firm and custodial or maintenance people, and we'll accumulate a chest full of tools of the trade. And we need some control over these tools, and possibly some vehicles. These chapters deal with that element of our management endeavor.

Nor will we ignore a building owner—the nonlicensee overseeing his or her own property directly, without the help of a management company. We welcomed these principals to come along for a ride through the text in the introductory chapter. Those readers may only manage one building, probably won't have their own maintenance staff and therefore may have to go into the labor market more often to keep their building rolling smoothly. The text may help them run the place more efficiently and economically.

We didn't plan it this way, but our words will be split between our two types of buildings, two options within our leases and two types of janitorial service, and all that suits us "two" a tee.

In the janitorial language, the office building will receive the early attention, but we won't ignore the strip center in later text. And we don't promise a how-to text for custodial work, down to a grade of wax for vinyl floors and the dilution ratio for the Pine-Sol in the restrooms. For that information please consult the vendors that supply the products for your application.

The janitorial staff is usually in the bright beam of the management spotlight, as their function is a daily ritual and is scrutinized by the totality of occupants and employees in the building or center. But as you read these pages, don't forget the others we employ that escape this degree of scrutiny: the jack-of-all-trades repairmen, the landscapers, painters and window washers. Our words, for the most part, apply to them also.

The Lease Obligation

In our textbook office building, with two or three tenants on each of three or four floors, we mathematically foresee 6 to 12 tenants who need nightly trash removal and cleaning services performed within their demised area. We need similar attention to the lobbies, rest-rooms, coffee-break rooms, stairwells and other common areas within the building.

Generally, we attempt to provide such service as an obligation of our lease, motivated by the fact that we don't particularly want 6 to 12 different janitorial firms, of each tenant's choosing, entering the building and a like number of front-door keys out to their employees, all utilizing sinks and facilities in the janitorial rooms and getting in each other's way. Unless a tenant is a complete stinker about security and after-hours access to their premises by your janitorial contractor, we're better off to suggest (or *demand!*) that we supply their custodial service.

Contract or Employed Labor?

Two options are available for labor: We can hire our own people and purchase the tools and supplies necessary to clean our building, or we can negotiate with a service to perform similar duties. Within these pages we'll not advocate one over the other—there's a lot of "case-basis" thinking to do on this score.

If we hire the custodians, we know who will be there every night, and we can communicate with them directly. The alternative is to deal with personnel of the contractor's choosing, each of whom is dis-patched sometimes to our property and other times to another and ar-rive at 8 P.M. one night and midnight the next in response to the contractor's priorities.

On the other hand, by using contract maintenance we enjoy some redundancy. If our own employee doesn't show up, we're stuck. The contractor has some depth of staff (or at least *should*—that's one pre-contract determination to make) and can cover us on a regular basis.

With contract maintenance we don't have an upfront outlay for custodial equipment. A decent commercial vacuum starts at a cool grand; we need more than enough buckets, squeegees and other nickel-and-dime items to double that outlay—and our experience is that it all tends to disappear from the building quite fast if unattended by management.

A manager is destined to have a *lot* of conversation with somebody over the quality of cleaning taking place or procedure updates in an office building. A major factor in that decision is whether you choose to talk during the day to a middleman, or at night directly to your own employee. But talk you will.

Custodial Supplies

Most of us don't have a clue how many cases of paper towels or tissues are used in a building with a given number of employees during a given period of time. There are two ways to arrive at a figure. The first way is to entertain bids from janitorial contractors to supply service *and supplies* for our building and let the service figure out how much to budget for the occupant load we enumerate in the bid request. The second way, if we plan to hire our own personnel, is to rely on the expertise of a local janitorial products supply firm. They have a good handle on estimating the quantities of paper products and floor-treatment and cleaning supplies we'll need.

We emphasized including supplies when inviting bids from outside contractors for another reason: If *we* buy the supplies for our contractors to place in dispensers throughout the building, we run the risk of involuntarily supplying a handful of other buildings that that janitorial firm cleans. When one of their other accounts is out of hand towels, it's awfully easy to take a case from our building that night to supply them—but a replacement case seldom comes back the next day. If paper products are included in our monthly bill, we don't care where they come up with them.

The Dumpster

The dumpster is another area for abuse by the general public, building employees and contract janitorial contractors. The public knows no shame when trash is being transported in the family wagon in search of a final resting place, and our building tenants' employees top this group. Most think one little kitchen-sized bag won't matter, but add enough little kitchen-sized bags, plus a few cartons and a box spring or mattress, and the thing's full.

A few building managers require their janitorial people to remove trash from the premises as part of their contract. If your custodial contractor has such an account, the chances are excellent that trash from that account will find its way into your dumpster. We hate to do it, but from time to time, when our dumpsters are loaded to the brim two days after the pickup day, we sift through the contents and invariably find another building's trash nestled among ours.

A padlock on the dumpster keeps the tenants out. A stern conversation of the we-weren't-born-yesterday nature with the janitorial firm can resolve the incursions from that quarter.

Reread the words of the "Access" chapter about padlocks: Make sure the trash-disposal-service truck has a key to the dumpster.

Uniforms

The text is still in the custodial phase, but the words that follow also apply to the other personnel who do work in our centers and offices. We choose the word *uniform* advisedly, as that implies a head-to-toe ensemble, when all we really need is a distinctive smock, T-shirt or baseball cap silk-screened with the building or janitorial firm's name to validate a person's presence in the building.

To put this into perspective, we offer the scenario of a lone employee working late in an office, confronted by an unidentified stranger walking in the back door. This sight, in today's America, is not a welcome one, but recognition of a distinctive cap or an inexpensive one-size-fits-all shirt puts the building occupant's mind at ease.

Somewhat in the uniform vein: safety equipment. The usual variants are hard hats or lightweight "bump caps" and safety-toe shoes, associated more with construction than with maintenance, and safety glasses and eardrum protection for those operating landscaping equipment and power tools. All cost a fraction of the cost of repairing an employee and are frequently mandated by your worker's compensation insurance.

Most management firms buy the first protection appliance for an employee; thereafter they are at the employee's expense, but they must wear them!

The Lone Employee

The subtitle doesn't cue Tonto and the William Tell overture, or a masked data-entry clerk working overtime at a computer screen. Years ago a janitor in our direct employ requested that we ask our building's tenants to require at least two female employees to work together, if office work had to be done into the evening hours. Thought through, the request had some merit, and we learned years later that this requirement has been standard procedure by some employers and office-building operators for many years.

We recounted the tale at a seminar, and learned that a California building manager hired a young lady to work alone as a custodian in a small building. She did an excellent job, but that didn't work out well either: Male employees, working after hours, felt some trepidation about potential, albeit far-flung, consequences.

Avoid any regulations that could possibly raise the specter of harrassment. Voices warn us that we're writing of thoughts displaying a discriminatory character, by the mere mention of gender. No such intention is meant, nor are any conclusions reached or solutions offered—the simple fact is that laws can be enacted and affirmations be made, but in human settings common sense must prevail.

This one suggestion is offered without apprehension: Work with your tenants to adopt a policy requiring more than one person, gender unspecified, to work in the building during evening hours if such work is necessary.

Polygraph Testing

There are in the world a number of employers who have a sort of "implied consent" clause in their applications for employment, giving them the right to demand, with or without cause, that their employees accept a polygraph test either to determine whether company assets were removed from company facilities or for a number of other situations.

We have encountered two such tenants, who in the broader interpretation of this thought demanded that our janitors, since they too had access to their facilities, be subjected to the same requirement.

We don't write these words to draw a conclusion. Both these occurrences happened to us a decade ago, and the issue was inflammatory even then. It hasn't got any better ten years later, and in modern thinking polygraph tests have been lumped under the same umbrella with employee drug testing, an emerging subject with unstable legal implications that we'll express no opinion about in these pages.

Our purpose in including this segment is to forewarn you that the subject exists and that it's coming your way sooner or later. In a very few instances we remind ourselves that we are an agent of a principal, and in certain matters high on the totem pole of civic perception or civil rights, we defer to our principal's counsel. This matter is one such.

*   *   *   *

Thus far in the chapter, the words have been mostly of our custodial crews, nocturnal sorts working inside, alone and unseen by most of the building population. We're expanding our personnel chapter now to the ladies and gentlemen who come out by daylight to maintain the interior and exterior of our buildings.

They Get Around

Our text is about small properties and property-management firms, so we can assume that the person who fixes sprinklers at one building we manage will probably work on several others—there isn't enough work in one small building to keep a person busy. Other prevalent categories of labor maintenance are painters, landscape and mowing crews, "deep" cleaning crews (who concentrate on areas within the properties that janitors have trouble cleaning during evening hours) and finally trash and rubbish collectors, who drive from property to property picking up trash and dumping litter barrels.

These people should also be identified by distinctive uniforms— they enter tenant areas. And they all need tools. A sharp property manager accounts for hand tools used by maintenance labor and from time to time conducts an inventory to confirm their existence and condition. Most of us managers spray-paint them with some ungodly neon color the instant they leave the hardware store so we can spot them in a private vehicle on a one-way journey out of our lives forever.

Employment by Tenants

An area of minor irritation for most property-management firms is the tendency of tenants to employ the property's maintenance people for some "little job" that invariably takes the employee out of circulation for a half a day, consumes a carton full of hardware from the property's stockpile and incites a hue and cry from every other tenant. "Susie brought in the center's big stepladder to water the plants and clean the skylights next door. Could you send her over here tomorrow to hang our mistletoe?"

Almost all management maintenance people cash in on their familiarity with our tenants and heed the tenant's request to take care of some minor construction for them—usually some task like putting up shelves, moving furniture or light carpentry and painting. Several problems exist: The first is insurance. An installation by a person in our employ could be construed as a lessor-supplied improvement or betterment, and if it crashed down and injured someone the liability could wind up in our laps.

Another reason is just plain simple: The employee can't work for us and the tenant at the same time. These litle "favor" side jobs occasionally drag out for several hours, during which time the employee is probably on our time clock. To combat this, we require employees who choose to perform work for tenants to do so after their regular shift. Even then, if they're in uniform, which we endorsed earlier as a good idea, we require the uniform to come off. Reason? Other tenants, seeing our uniformed employee performing a chore for one tenant, think they too are entitled to have the same chore done in their premises. Sans the uniform, the cord to property management is cut—or at least frayed.

Use of Company Equipment

We'll leave this to your judgment, but we urge that some policy be in place. Frankly, we have little problem with an employee using a company buzz saw while working for a tenant on his or her own time, but we'd be a little peeved if the employee took the company pickup to the junkyard with a load of trash. The value, operating cost and potential liability arising out of use of the equipment figures heavily into this judgment. And in any case, we want to know in advance about noncompany use of any asset bigger than a hand tool.

And in the same vein, we hate to get too miserly over minor supplies like a handful of 16-penny nails or an electrical wall box, but they all do add up, and in truth they're the asset of the building owner, also known as our boss. We therefore preach a little fire and brimstone about disappearing company property once in a while, to let all concerned know that we're not unaware of the silent misappropriation of the stuff.

Power Equipment.   In an individual small building, we're likely to find some gasoline or electric-powered equipment such as snowblowers, lawn mowers and trimmers and push-type sweepers. On the management-company plateau, some similar equipment, but a little bigger: snowplows, gang mowers, riding sweepers, "scissors," high-lift platforms or cherry pickers, lifts, compressors and airless paint sprayers. And not strictly power equipment, but in the same vein, are trailers: utility trailers and platform trailers to haul all this equipment around on from property to property. A larger property might merit a pickup truck with a towbar or a plow.

Most of this equipment can hurt someone, or seriously damage property if used incorrectly. For this reason, we need a procedure to certify our people in the safe operation of power equipment, and we maintain a written list of who is approved to operate it.

Interproperty Loans

Inevitably, the owner of the center across the street is going to take a serious interest in your snowplow, and since he's the proud owner of a 30-foot snorkel, you're more than happy to send the plow across the street for a couple of hours to tidy things up for your neighbor, because that snorkel lift sure beats a shaky old ladder for changing your parking-lot light bulbs.

The first consideration is getting the plow across the street. Frequently such equipment is not licensed or insured to travel on public streets. We can sneak it over, but that's not good business. The better way is to consult your insurance agent about coverage available for this type of equipment.

A second consideration is the operator of the machine. We'd sooner send our own employee to work the plow than loan it to our neighbor's untrained operator. A couple of hours extra on our payroll won't hurt us, we'll get the machine back in one piece and the responsibility is clearly defined if something does go wrong.

On-Premises Fuel Storage

As the number of gasoline-powered machines used on the premises grows, so grows the need to get rid of some gas cans—and the fumes and spills and trips to the station they require—by installing a small below-ground gasoline tank with a light-duty pump and meter.

The benefits are many, most implied in the paragraph above, with the additional benefit of quantity purchasing and exemption from the fuel tax tacked on in some areas for vehicles using public streets. The drawback to a private pump is obvious—fuel from the tank has a way of seeking a path into employees' cars if a tight system isn't set up to account for dispensing it.

"Nonowned Auto" Insurance

This short gem could go in a number of chapters, but we choose to put it with discussions about employees because an employee or contractor frequently uses his or her own vehicle while working for us.

Most comprehensive general liability insurance policies (the form that your owner probably has on the property you manage) offer "nonowned auto" as a coverage. It's inexpensive, and it covers the ownership's third-party liability if an employee causes property damage or bodily injury to another while using a personal car in the conduct of your business *on the premises*. (The author is a real estate broker, not an insurance agent, so verify your needs with your local agent!)

Retaining Good Employees

We've taken a few people aboard our management team, either as our own employees or as independent contractors. If they're to be our own employees, and their duties take them into tenant territory, we need to think about fidelity bonding. And we need to keep them insured by a worker's compensation policy. They'll need training and uniforms, the latter maybe supplied by a uniform service that cleans the clothes also.

We want to retain our employees on our payroll—the choice of benefits to offer them is yours, but consider it well: A Ford Tempo

comes off the line, identical to the ones ahead of it and following behind. But your building is unique, so much so that the architect's
plans usually vary from the finished product, and the employee who
has the place figured out and can operate it for you is an asset. A good
employee who knows the tenants' names and enjoys a rapport with
them is a valuable person to keep. A contribution to an employee
group-health insurance program and a reasonable holiday and vaca-
tion compensation plan pay for themselves by reducing our labor
turnover.

A former college roommate who recently had a book dedicated to
him now owns the most successful property-management firm in Nevada and carries forward today a nice touch he started when he
opened the doors to his firm in 1973: Some of the most powerful people in the state work each day in the buildings his firm manages. He
hosts a party each year, and now, as then, they all come to the party,
where they share holiday cheer with the gardeners, the security
guards, the janitors and the painters—the entire rank-and-file of the
firm. Wild horses couldn't drag these employees away from his company.

11

Leases

An entomologist friend of ours who operates a research facility in the Santa Susana mountains north of Los Angeles was contacted by the California Cotton Growers Association a few years ago. They were attempting to obtain specimens of a particularly voracious beetle that was ravaging their crops in the San Joaquin Valley.

She had only two of that species, so she was reluctant to sell them, but she did offer to loan them to the association, for a fee.

And she's been known by all ever since then as the Lessor of Two Weevils.

*　　*　　*　　*

The astute reader may ask why a chapter on revenue generation, a function so integral to ownership of property, has been relegated to the October days of the book, following some topics that are, on balance, relatively minor.

Our response would be that the book is basically of property management, and we'll all come to learn when we start playing with the big kids in the commercial real estate industry that the property managers are frequently about three floors away, or clear across town, from the leasing department.

The disciplines are totally different. Leasing is a marketing function, differing little from the function of any other merchant. Grocers sell food, bankers sell money, airlines sell seats and leasing agents sell space, and all watch their competitors. When Safeway or Delta changes its prices, Alpha Beta or United scrambles. And if the office plaza across the street advertises a month's free rent, the other leasing agents adjust to the competition.

Management people, by contrast, are not competition-oriented. Our buzzwords are economy of building operation and maintenance, continuity and consistency of service and maximizing the net revenue. The leasing agent maximizes the *gross* rental revenue, we hang onto as much of it as we can for the owner.

A fair number of us in the business never have the pleasure of referring a prospective tenant to a leasing agent or telling the tenant with a leaking roof to call the property manager. In the size of building we address in the book, we do it all, and much of the language in the property-management segment of the book has been to provide managers with facts for informing prospective tenants of the buildings amenities when our leasing agent hats are on.

The Scope of the Chapter

We're not trying, during the next few pages, to rewrite one of the great existing written compendia of leasehold theory. Besides, we find considerable regional variations in lease marketing. What we *are* going to do is put some information from the leasing texts into the context of a light retail or office occupancy.

Take note that when two great powers come together to "lease and hire" space in a major center, a roomful of attorneys and CPAs will massage the lease form all over the table before it is executed. (In one case in Reno a Fortune top-10 company's team still forgot to demand snow removal from the lessor!) In this book championing small-building and roll-up-your-sleeves management, most of the negotiation for a small retail bay or office space is between you and the prospective tenant. We endorse the final opinion of an attorney, but the following phraseology is geared to those who must be self-reliant.

Noncompete Clauses

In the next few categories, the relative strengths of the prospective tenant and the center foretell whether either's desire for a *noncompete* or *noncompetition* clause in the lease will be realized.

The *noncompete* clause, in simplest terms, is a warranty by the lessor that it will not subsequently place another tenant into the center that would constitute substantial competition for the benefactor of the clause.

For example: A sunglass shop in our town holds the right to sell quality sunglasses in one mall. An aviation supply store moved into the mall but is enjoined from selling Ray-Ban glasses, even though that brand is synonymous with aviation.

Some good sense is necessary in granting and enforcing these clauses: In the same mall, a discount drug store sells costume grade (under $10) glasses, not considered to be significant competition to Ray-Ban, Vuarnet and Porsche products.

We are constantly confronted with requests for such clauses, and must use foresight rivaling a crystal ball to avoid granting an exclusive right to a tenant, at the risk of discouraging a stronger tenant from taking space in the center at a later date. One key is a tight definition of the restricted product. "Shoe" doesn't make it—there are a dozen types and we don't want to give one tenant a headlock on the center. Spell it out: outdoor, dress, athletic, uniform, snow or brake. Look well down the road for possible conflicts.

What happens if the aviation store decides to sell Ray-Bans anyway, in contravention of your lease? We won't speak for our attorneys, but experience has been that the sunglass shop holds us in breach for permitting the competitive occupancy, and we in turn hold the aviation store in breach for selling the glasses in violation of a prohibition that we put into the lease.

Fortunately, our buildings and beefs are smaller in scale, and just as it doesn't take a battery of attorneys to slug out a lease, we can handle such a breach on a face-to-face basis with the offending tenant. We indicated above that a manager may not be into *marketing*, but he or she definitely practices *salesmanship!*

Distance Clauses

Many successful centers include a "distance clause" in their leases, stating that a tenant cannot have *ownership of* or *use the same name as* any similar business within a certain radius of the subject center (usually three to five miles). Restated for clarity: The tenant can't own a store offering similar goods or services, with the same or a different name, within that distance; *nor* can the tenant operate under a name in use within that distance even if the ownership (e.g., another Hallmark franchise operated by another franchisee) is different.

The most obvious reason for including this limitation is that a center operator would like that center's name to become associated with a store, and the proximity of another store dilutes that intent.

A less obvious motivator for the clause is to prevent a store owner from referring a patron to another store location owned by the same entity where the rent is not determined by gross sales.

Many retail stores in gross-rent centers, and particularly stores selling high-ticket items like jewelry or firearms, maintain an alternate location where an interested customer may be sent to purchase an item that's "out of stock" at the more prominent location. The savings the merchant realizes on the mall gross rent easily compensates them for keeping the second location. (Next time you drive by a shopping center or a major hotel with an arcade of shops, note the second-rate little jewelry shop across the street: people wonder if it does any business—it does.)

The distance clause makes the merchant think twice about sending the customers out the door without the merchandise. That extra distance inconveniences the patrons and jeopardizes the sale.

Like-Business and Occupancy Clauses

The concept that a sunglass shop, a record and tape store and a computer center want to limit or eliminate competition within the center is not difficult to comprehend. After all, who *does* want competition? Jewelry stores, for one, and ladies' fashions and shoe stores, among others.

There are many types of merchants who don't want to be the *only* store in a center selling that line of product. They've determined that shoppers go where there's a selection of wares. (The auto industry, while not germane to this text, is proof positive of this—car lots group up like sheep. The manufacturers and distributors demand it.)

Other categories of merchants are less concerned with what type of stores open in the center, be they similar or unrelated to theirs, as long as plenty of warm bodies walk through the center attracted by a large number of tenants. They'll take their chances that the law of large numbers will send a share of shoppers their way.

The text exceeds what the typical small-mercantile-strip manager experiences, but it's worth reading: Larger and more desirable national and regional tenants often predicate their rent payments on the center occupancy, particularly in a new center while it's filling. A rental amount will be struck, based upon "full" (or at least 90 percent) occupancy. A factor is included to adjust the rental amount downward to correspond with less than full occupancy, and it may be adjusted upward or further down by the number of stores similar to the subject—dress stores *like* other dress stores, for example. The upward adjustment is a motivation for the leasing agent to cater to prospective tenants favorable to the dress store already in the center.

These clauses usually have relevance only while a new center fills. (Or empties, if it's in trouble.) An oversimplification might simply be "half-filled equals half-rent," followed by an upward adjustment of the rent as new tenants move in. The lessor, bound by language in the lease, is required to give accurate occupancy figures to the tenant.

This is the exotic stuff of the larger centers and malls, but every once in a while we find a major tenant interested in space in our modest little strip centers, and a slick "facilities acquisition manager" or some such supernumerary tries to slip such a clause into the lease. Our intent isn't to endorse a yea or nay—if your center's filling, the clause has only short-term impact, and that tenant may lure a few more tenants to the center. Our intent is simply to introduce you to the clause.

The Gross Lease

We used a term in that last segment that needs some embellishment: The term is *gross lease*, interchangeable with *percentage lease*. You'll hear both terms associated with retail rentals, and you'll encounter them both early in your career.

This type of lease creates a one-way partnership between the tenant and the lessor—if the tenant does well, the lessor does well also. If the tenant doesn't set the world on fire, the lessor is still assured a "base" rent.

The retail industry has developed a good "feel" for how much a particular type of store should make within a known set of demographics—market-area population, the income of that population, vehicle access to the center, competition proximate to the center and other, similar, factors. From this resource a sharp leasing agent can determine that an 18,000-square-foot men's big-and-tall shop in a given center should generate a minimum of $100,000 a month in gross sales, and from that projection base the rent at $1,000 per month. (All sales figures and percentages are intentionally random.)

In this hypothetical *percentage lease* language, the tenant will pay the minimum rent if sales fall below $100,000. The lease requires 5 percent of gross sales over $100,000 and up to $125,000, $2\frac{1}{2}$ percent of sales over $125,000 and up to $150,000, and 1 percent of any sales exceeding $150,000—all as additional rent. Thus, if the tenant in the example had a great month and sold $165,000 worth of XXL's, they would pay $1,000 (base rent) + $1,250 (5% of $25,000) + $625 ($2\frac{1}{2}$% of the next $25,000) + $150 (1% of $15,000), or a monthly rental of $3,025. Note that the example has several plateaus; other leases may have more or fewer, and we've seen a few where at some attainable sales level, the percentage sinks to zero, allowing the merchant to retain all that it sells above that ceiling.

The system is a subtle motivator for a merchant to strive to increase sales: The earlier in the month each plateau is passed, the greater the return to the tenant for the same dollar volume of business. Not so subtle is the fact that the success of the tenant builds the success of center ownership. The flattening curve is a nice touch; a reward for the tenant that merchandizes diligently.

And the contribution is not *all* bad for the tenant—center management and ownership is given an incentive to do a better job of merchandising the center as a whole at their own expense, given this opportunity to increase rental income through increased traffic.

Obtaining Valid Sales Figures.   The tenants, on a monthly or quarterly basis, file with your state a notarized document attesting to the total amount of taxable sales in the location. Our lease with them states that our auditor shall have access to this document for the purpose of promulgating rent. We don't care too much about the lines following "gross sales"—nontaxable sales are mildly interesting, but don't have a great bearing on our center. The "gross" line is the one we look at, then subject it to the percentages and plateaus in our lease, as we did in the men's shop example above.

Deception.   They may kid us, but few tenants would try to pull the wool over the state tax receiver's eyes by perpetrating a fraud against the state. Besides, their state tax filing probably becomes an exhibit in their federal tax return, which makes the consequences of fooling us tougher yet.

We know they may sell a $600 shotgun or two through their other store across town to customers that first saw them in our center, and we concede that lost lease revenue. But in the long run, the sales tax filings form a reliable indicator.

*   *   *   *

All this just scratches the surface of gross or percentage leases. They're a leasing and merchandising science unto themselves, and we urge you to dig deeper for local expertise if you get involved in the bigger malls.

The "Favored Tenant" Clause

We approach this clause with stealth, primarily because it needs a great deal more localized input and some fairly sophisticated unraveling from both the legal and marketing standpoints. We'll touch lightly on the clause, just so you'll recognize the term and the intent. Note that we've been in the retail center context for a few pages; this topic returns us to retail *and* office tenancies.

Some tenants, these usually the heavyweights, want assurance that they are not paying more rent than any other tenant in the complex. And this may be interpreted as *current* rent or as rent at some time in the future.

It's a fair request, a bargaining chip we can live with or deny, balancing what benefits come along with the restraints they entail.

But choose your qualifiers wisely: The usual grief occurs after we establish their rent at a dollar a foot a month for 2,500 square feet, and warrant that it's the lowest in the building, which it may be. Then along comes a tenant that wants a whole floor, 12,000 square feet, and we know that all other things being equal, per-foot rent usually shrinks as the leased space rises. We put them in for 75 cents a foot, and barring language to the contrary, have to apply the lower rent to the 2,500-foot tenant as well.

The key to these clauses is comparing apples to apples: Cite in the lease language any variables that could cloud the clause. These could be space variation, construction costs amortized into a lease, desirability of the space (view, foot traffic), parking spaces alloted and a few others you may foresee within your building.

The favored-tenant clause is a valid concept, and you'll hear it requested by your majors. We've told you what it *is*; get a local pro to tell you how it *works* in your area!

Escalator Clauses

You'll hear the phrase "a five-year lease with an annual escalator." The *escalator* is the formula that's *known by both parties* at the inception of the lease, by which the rental amounts may be periodically adjusted up or down. We seldom know what the dollar figure will be past the first year, but for the lease to be enforceable, a formula, if not the dollar amount, must be recited.

We'll skip the obvious escalators that justify little discussion, for example "an increase of five percent each year," and also skip the exotic clauses tied to some crazy formula of demographics that only a PhD in marketing can fathom. What does need some attention is a term thrown around constantly in the leasing business: *C.P.I. increase.* Many agents use it, but not as many tenants understand it. We'd like you to finish this book with fundamental knowledge of the term and the formula.

C.P.I. is *Consumer Price Index*, a market-basket survey taken by the U.S. Department of Commerce of the costs of all the things and services we consumers typically buy. It's seasonally adjusted, e.g., furnace oil cost is surveyed in the winter but omitted during the summer when no market for it exists. The index is published every two months and is localized to a number of major population areas. It's properly expressed in a lease as the "Consumer Price Index, All Products and Service, (your area) region as of March 1, 19____." As a matter of information, there are other indexes published, of less value to us, such as wholesale price, maritime, agricultural and a few others. We'll stick with "consumer" in these pages.

The common misconception is that the C.P.I. is a percentage telling property managers how much to raise (or lower) their tenants' leases, and it just doesn't work that way. To avoid problems with tenants, it is important to tell them how the index will be applied to their rent on each anniversary of their lease (the usual time to apply escalators).

The index is a *number*, lately three digits, at this writing in the low 100s. It changes, up or down, every two months—in inflationary times, the market basket costs more, so the number rises.

When we sign a lease with a C.P.I. escalator, we include language stating that the parties agree that the index published closest to the execution of the lease is "_____" (insert the number from the index).

At the first anniversary of the lease, we obtain the current index from the Department of Commerce. That current index is divided by the index established at inception.

Example: The inception index was 132. Inflation has occurred, and a year later the index is 154. 154 divided by 132 equals 1.17, interpreted in the lease language as a 17 percent raise in the tenant's rent.

Several Notes: We structured the example to make a point. That rate of inflation is high, at a level that was not experienced even during the inflationary period of the early 1980s. The point is that we may include other language to further define the application of the C.P.I. indicator and agree that the increase *shall not exceed* x *percent of current rent* in any one lease year. (A 5 percent limit would cap the 17 percent increase.) Or we may agree that application of the C.P.I. *shall never result in a reduction of rent*.

This is a stable indicator, well defined and understood by most leasing professionals. It may form only a part of the escalator clause—in some leases, any increases in real property taxes or other expenses are added to the escalator, in fact as a pass-through and not resulting in any additional income for the lessor.

The escalator clause is integral to the next clause on the menu, the *option to renew*. We should probably alert you to this book's Index, in which you may retrieve items from this segment's barrage of terminology.

The Option To Renew

Very few leases indeed fail to offer the tenant the opportunity to renew the lease for some stated period of time (but not necessarily the same interval as the original lease term). Some leases offer a number of options, e.g., a five-year initial lease with *two* three-year options. We're not going to explore options in textbook depth, but a few rudimentary points should be made for the benefit of the building owner or agent doing leasing as an adjunct to property-management duties.

Rental Amount.   The first trap that many fall into is to offer an option without a clearly defined method for determining the rental amount during the option period. The states are unanimous in the requirement that, to be enforceable, *an option must include the renewal rental amount, or a formula to determine that amount.*

Dollars are an excellent way of expressing rent, but it's tough to come up with a fair figure for an event that takes place five years in the future. We can go back to our old friend of several paragraphs ago, the C.P.I. in effect at that time as compared with that index today. That's a formula, using a resource with continuity, and that meets legal criteria.

But *don't* offer an option "at a rental amount to be agreed upon by the parties at the inception of the option." That language would be unenforceable—the parties may not agree. (A valuable thought to remember when dealing with contracts that take five or ten years to perfect is that the present owner of the building may sell it, the tenant could assign the lease or you may be gone. Don't count on personal charm to get the job done. Your next principal or tenant could be a real piranha.

Notice of Intent.   Another clause we want in the option is one that requires the tenant to give us notice of intent to exercise the option at least two or three months prior to the expiration of the original lease. We don't need the pins and needles of awaiting their verdict right down to the last day of the lease before we can make arrangements to rehabilitate the space and advertise to relet it.

We can accomplish our aim of adequate notice either by an explicit clause in the lease requiring it or by a *holding-over* clause, defining the rights and obligations of a tenant who continues to occupy the premises past the expiration of the lease. A tenant may merrily sail through Friday when the lease is expiring Sunday, then open for business on Monday morning as if everything's just fine. If such tenants-at-sufferance tender the former rent and we accept it, they are our legal tenant for at least 30 more days.

If, however, we establish in the lease a *holdover rental payment* amount outrageously high enough to get their attention, we might bring them to the table in time to work out a more businesslike arrangement.

*   *   *   *

A final minor note is to avoid using terminology like "an option to renew for five years at the same terms and conditions as this lease." One of those "same terms" in the lease is the option to renew itself, and granting "the same terms" extends the option to perpetuity. Courts have grudgingly snuffed these out, but the better language adds "save for rental payments and the right to further options to renew."

Assignments and Subtenancies

By definition, an assignment of lease is the act of one party ceding their leasehold interest in real property, in total, to another party. The assignment document requires three signatures: the original tenant, quitclaiming all right and interest to the premises; the new tenant, accepting all the terms and conditions of the existing lease; and finally the lessor (or agent: you!), acceding to the change in tenancy.

Several thoughts are appropriate here: In most states, the legal right to assign a lease may not be withheld from a tenant *arbitrarily and capriciously*, the usual language in most state statutes. In general practice, an entity with *credit* equal to or exceeding that of the original tenant must be accepted as an assignee.

Another barometer is the *use* of the premises—in an office setting, an assignee is a logical and acceptable replacement tenant if he or she has a comparable number of employees, requires the same number of parking spaces, creates a similar number of vehicle trips due to deliveries and whatnot and meets other similar commonsense criteria.

To withhold the assignment, the lessor generally needs to prove that the assignee would denigrate the property through an adverse use of the premises. A real estate office assigning its lease to an insurance office would be tough to prevent; in a center, a shoe repair store assigning to a jet-engine test facility would be preventable.

We get quite a few requests for assignments, and each requires some thought.

Tradestyles and Franchises.   An area to consider when faced with an assignment in a retail center is the ownership of a franchise or tradestyle that might in fact have been the strongest reason to rent to the original tenant.

A retail landlord may or may not rent to Karl Breckenridge predicated on credit, references or the financial statement, but if he owned a Hallmark franchise, most would rent to him in a heartbeat.

When this book is done, we'll give a copy to one of our favorite owner/principals, and he'll read then that we didn't run a credit check on a prospective tenant for one of his buildings, a Kawasaki motorcycle dealer. We allowed that if the tenant was good enough for a national distributor like Kawasaki, they were good enough for us too. And we've had a cordial relationship for nine years.

We frequently encounter tenants who own the tradestyle or franchise of their business and choose to assign their leases to others; the assignee in truth runs the business for the owner. (The relationships are often far more complicated; we have greatly oversimplified for the sake of clarity.)

We would be foolish to assign a lease to the franchisee and let the owner of the tradestyle off the hook, as the owner is our strongest single source of continuity of rent. In the retail setting, if we're dealing with a chain or franchise, we keep the lease in the name of the franchise holder, and let that entity do whatever they will with other operators.

A footnote to this assignment segment: Pay particular attention to funds being held as advance rent, last month's rent, damage or any other form of deposit. The lessor holds these monies as a credit to someone's account—the time to determine who that entity is, is at the time of assignment. This information should be included on the assignment document when it's executed by the parties.

The Sublet.   An entity (office or retail), presently needing 3,000 square feet of space, but anticipating the need for 10,000 square feet of space within the next five years, leases that larger space in our building.

They then advertise to sublease the remaining 7,000 feet to another party on a three-year lease with a couple of one-year options.

We, as property managers, have the right to approve this sublet, and we subject the request to criteria similar to those governing an assignment.

What's important to us is continuity—if the tenant is required to carry insurance, we want the same from the subtenant. Ditto on the parking rules, weekend use of the office, window displays in retail centers and so on.

One document that differs from other common leasing paperwork is this one: The subtenant may come to you, requesting you as the lessor to execute a document known in most circles as a *right of quiet enjoyment*, guaranteeing the subtenant that if *their landlord*, who is synonymous with *your tenant*, commits any act that would jeopardize the underlying lease (failure to pay rent comes to mind), that you, the prime lessor, will grant the subtenant the right to cure the existing default and continue their tenancy in the same form and fashion as a direct tenant of yours. Consistent with granting this request is an obligation for you to notify them of any default of the tenant's, concurrently with notice to the tenant.

*   *   *   *

This chapter, a long one, is offered as a collection of notes for building managers crossing over to the leasing-agent side of light commercial real estate, and we've boxed them up as a break-glass-in-case-of-a-leasing-emergency resource. We hope that you'll enhance your familiarity with leasing by consulting other textbooks.

We have some notes left over about leasing and property-management administrative activities, and other notes about tenant or merchant's associations. Since the merchant's association aligns with this leasing chapter, a minichapter about that falls next in line, followed by a look at the duties the property manager's office performs on a daily basis.

12

The Merchant's Association

While P.T. Barnum and the showrooms of Las Vegas rested on their laurels, the myriad of retail shopping centers' merchant's associations overtook and passed them as America's dominant talent-booking agencies.

Most of the entertainment that captivates weekend shoppers aren't ready to quit their day jobs yet, but the center provides a forum and a springboard to greater stages, and a few mall stars eventually do quite well!

*   *   *   *

This is less a chapter in its own right than an appendage to the retail leasing chapter and food for thought for the manager of a small retail center.

Many merchant's associations, or tenant's associations as they are sometimes called, are created by language in each lease, and execution of the lease acquiesces to membership in the association together with the responsibility of contributing dues. In some leases the association dues are collected as a part of rent and remitted by the lessor to the association's treasurer.

A merchant's association is a worthwhile endeavor for those in any retail complex, lessor and lessee alike, from our small strip center to the major hundred-tenant regional malls where the business of the association is conducted in an office in the mall with several full-time employees. Large or small, their purposes are the same: To collect one dollar from each tenant, in hope of giving them back five or ten or a hundred dollars in increased sales—and to speak as one unified voice to the center's ownership.

Center Advertising

One of the major functions of the association is the administration of an advertising program, showcasing the center as a whole. Many centers, even the smaller ones, have an advertising representative, and dues, together with contributions from the lessor and ''co-op'' contributions from the tenants' wholesale distributors, are pooled to create a direct-mail promotion or a newspaper supplement, for example.

(Co-op, or cooperative advertising, is the contribution or compensation paid by a manufacturer to a retail outlet for advertising that manufacturer's product. If you see a local store advertising a Sylvania television, bet that Sylvania paid a part of that ad.)

Readerboard Scheduling

In the ''Signs and Visuals'' chapter we suggested that the association bear the burden of telling us what to put up on the board, and those words are echoed here. The tenants can discuss among themselves who gets the board next, and what their message will be. We're thereby spared the appearance of playing favorites.

Tenant Meetings

If we're to achieve harmony on the advertising and the readerboards, we'd better get together as a group from time to time. It's nice if one tenant, such as a restaurant, has room for all the other tenants, and we usually supply the beverages and snacks as a peace offering. We may attend to assist them, or we may be absent so they can meet among themselves, if they prefer that option. To conduct the meeting and keep the minutes, they elect officers.

Association Officers

The association is a business unto itself, usually with a bank account, some commercial credit accounts with printers and advertising media and other local businesses, and it therefore needs a slate of officers: at least a president to conduct meetings, a secretary to keep minutes and a treasurer to account for the cash rolling in. A major function is a creative–public relations type who can dream up new events to hold in the center and who knows what community buttons to push to bring them there.

Common Area Events

There are, all over your town, groups and clubs and choirs and youth functions and health fairs looking for a place out of the rain with 110-volt power to hold a public-service event. And shoppers love these events.

The association's function is to seek out these organizations, or evaluate the organizations that seek them out, for their appeal to the shopping public and desirability in the center. As managers, we don't want to give some medieval historical society *carte blanche* to recreate an English countryside joust with real horses and lances in the space between the Radio Shack and B. Dalton's side door, so we might want to retain the ultimate say over these matters.

These can be great business builders, so we include them on the readerboard and accumulate some supplies and props, a small moveable stage and an old spinet piano to facilitate such use.

And this is not only the stuff of the larger centers or malls—even in our small strip centers we have a paved parking lot, which is all some groups need to put on a show. Take our advice: Get your local National Guard unit to park one (1) Abrams tank there on a Saturday morning as a recruiting ploy, and you'll have kids dragging shopping mothers with credit cards to your mall, a crowd second only to the crowd on the morning that Santa arrives in the Guard's Huey chopper.

Common Area Facilities and Services

We should note that the tenants' association is not reserved for retail tenants, but exists on a smaller scale in many office complexes.

Whether in an office or a retail building, the association is indispensable in first reaching accord among the tenants and then communicating to the lessor their accord regarding common area services and facilities.

As lessors, we provide facilities and services to our tenants at a number of levels: The lowest level is whatever we have to do to get certificated for occupancy by the city. That's only basic life safety—pretty thin. The next level is providing the amenities necessary to make our centers attractive and competitive, to draw tenants. Those are elective activities, and they dress up the appearance and make the place a nicer destination for shoppers or office workers.

We get into the area at a higher level when our expenditures do not benefit all tenants equally, and this is the threshold where we stop and ask for the tenants' input. We don't mind spending the money to accommodate the tenant's wishes, but we'd like to respond to a *consensus* of all the tenants, not just a few. The association is the body we look to for this input.

At some point, we don't want to spend any more money on *anything*—we feel that we've provided a safe, attractive and well-equipped property, and further improvements must come from the tenants themselves. In meeting among themselves, if a majority of them feel that they want piped music and a paging system or an interior readerboard or some other amenity or service, they are free to purchase it, we'll install it and they can collect payment for it among themselves.

In most associations, all tenants are bound by the majority's vote. They usually are assessed for extra costs on the basis of the percentage of their leased floor space in relation to the total space of the center. In such cases, the bookkeeping and the collection is the function of the association, not the lessor (manager).

The Tenant Mix

The people who know more about what the center needs than we do are the people already in the center—the merchants who are continually asked by shoppers where in the center they may find a typewriter ribbon or manila file folders. There's a trend forming here: Maybe the center needs a stationery store.

Balancing the tenant "mix" in a center is an art form, a study in the disposable income of the shoppers, their age and gender and the proper balance of goods and services. We've been to major centers where all the men are in one wing of the center and the women in another; everybody in one wing is eating fast food and walnut-paneled restaurants dominate another; all in one area are cowboys, in another we see spiked hair and chains, and around the corner all shoppers are pushing babies in strollers. We've heard that this is by design, and that stores are grouped to promote this segregation. We won't venture an opinion on right or wrong—one of the nation's major shopping center owners also owns an NFL football team of some note and we don't, so far be it from us to Monday-morning-quarterback their decisions.

What does fall to us as property managers is the location of your tenants within the center, and as vacancies occur, we seek the input of the merchant's association about what type of store the center management should entertain and where best to locate it if there's a choice.

The Newsletter

We include the newsletter in the "tenant association" context partly because we rely on that association to provide material for our office building's or shopping center's paper. In truth we regard the publishing of a paper or newsletter a management function. It includes news of people and events in the center, in the surrounding neighborhood, new tenants, tenants' employees and product lines.

But it's also the greatest little management tool that's come down the pike for communicating with the tenants' matters as minor as the fire lane that's going to be torn up and repaved next month, as important as the lot striping that must be done and the need to relocate parked cars, and as foreboding as the serious tail-twisting that's going to take place if tenants don't start collapsing cartons before they go into the dumpster. (Such promise of certain mayhem, delivered to *all* tenants, is a nonthreatening but effective warning to the one or two that we're really targeting.)

A tenant newsletter is a cheap vehicle to bond the tenants and employees together, to keep them informed and otherwise to perform a

significant amount of management while doing nothing more strenu-
ous than sitting in front of a typewriter.

*   *   *   *

And speaking of sitting in front of a typewriter, we'll leave the tenant's
association topic and go now to the management office, where we
keep the typewriter and a few other tools and files that we use to run
this building. The text isn't about office procedure, but we do have a
few salient pointers to pass on in this next mini-chapter.

13

Administration

The management office is the nerve center of any building, its occupants the first to hear the news and rumors of impending disaster. One day, while we set timers following the end of Daylight Savings Time, a bantering tenant came close to convincing us that there would be one less hour of daylight than there was the day prior. Prolonged exposure to the management office can soften the mind to the point that a one-hour adjustment to the solar system seemed almost reasonable.

*   *   *   *

In this chapter we invite readers to picture in their mind's eye an office where property management and leasing is done. It may be a real estate brokerage office, with the records of our small building on handwritten files comprising half a desk drawer, or you may visualize a suite in an urban high-rise tower, where our building is known by a five-digit code in a major property-management company's computer. It matters not—we have the same job to do in either environment. We'll spare you any extended text on office procedures. What's happening here is an enumeration of a few topics to think about in connection with managing the building.

We're dividing the text into three categories of actions we take: Those triggered by a chronology of events; those related to revenue generation through rental payments and finally management-related expenses.

Trigger Events

An obvious event in the life of a property manager or a tenant is the first of the month, the day we pay or receive rent. (For many of us, the day we do both!)

How, you say, *could that be of any import in a book?* We thank you for that question from the floor and we'll tell you why: Many property managers lease a space in an office or a center on a given date, say the 13th of the month, and base the lease on that date, anticipating a rental payment on the 13th of every month during the life of the lease.

If only one space is being leased, that's fine, but most of us have a tub full of ledger cards or a field on the IBM for each tenant, and rent day is the first of each month. As we receive rental payments, we so note on the ledger cards or the disk, and at any time during the month we can grab the ledger cards that remain on the unpaid side of the tub, or push a key on the computer and know that every tenant that appears is delinquent. But if every tenant in the place has a different lease date, one on the first, another on the fifth, and so on, and therefore a different delinquent date, we'd have to look at each card in the group of ledgers. Some would be delinquent, others would not owe yet.

The advice is to prorate the initial, or first month's rent for each tenant to take them to the first of the following month, and their rent is thereafter due each first day. And they'll seldom mind this proration—invariably they'll wind up paying less than a full month's rent early in the lease.

If your lease cites the *total* rent to be paid during the life of the lease, which a well-written lease should, a short memo to the lease file subsequent to execution of the lease memorializes that fact that one rental period was adjusted to prorate to the following month.

Late Rent.   The next usual chronological event is late rent. *Late* is a subjective word in this text—it may be statutory, cited in the lease language or both—but for our purposes we may put it in terms of pulling up a handful of ledger cards and considering those to be late.

The key word is *breach.* We give written notice to those tenants to cure the *default* within the statutory or contractual period. The form of that notice, like other notices we'll read of soon, might be personal delivery, posting of the premises or notification by first-class mail, postage prepaid. There may be two or more other statutory options—check the laws in your own state.

If that doesn't bring them to the office with a check, plan B in many states is the *Notice to Quit,* demanding that the premises be ceded to the owner or *in the alternative* to pay rent. In our western states we must grant the alternative at this level of breach.

Note that several actions have been taken, by letter, service or posting. What we really don't want, but what may become the final alternative, is eviction. And in most jurisdictions, documentation of this chain of events, with the best forms of proof possible, such as a photo of the notice on the premise's door or a witness's affidavit of the personal service, should be available to take to court or to whatever judiciary body hears eviction cases in your area.

Eviction.   In our book destined to reach the 50 states, the free world and ships at sea we're not going to put our neck in a noose by describing eviction procedure, which varies from commercial to residential tenancy, state to state and occasionally, in our state, from judge to judge.

Suffice it to say that eviction is the closing aria of the unpaid rent operetta, and at the close of this act you as manager get to catalog the evictee's personal property, admit half the businesses in the Yellow Pages to retrieve the evictee's leased assets *(after ownership is documented!)* and feed the fish in the waiting room or call animal control to take the parrot to a new home (author's personal experience). It's all personal property and must be protected.

A Calendaring System.   Every holiday season we receive a bunch of attractive wall and pocket calendars, but giving a property manager a 12-month calendar is akin to giving the Chicago Bears' "Fridge" Perry a chicken drumstick—the calendar and the drumstick don't go very far. What we're looking for is a ten-year *Far Side* calendar, with weird humor stretched out to the coming millennium.

And what would we put on it? The encapsulation of our leases, some reaching to or exceeding ten years when escalator clauses are involved.

The dates of expiration of our leases and the dates that escalators can be exercised should be calendared. We plan on making the statement in the coming "Setting Up a New Account" chapter that many property managers sail blithely past these escalation dates without raising the rents.

Options To Renew.   Most leases contain an option to renew, and our counsel in an earlier chapter was to corner a tenant into committing to renew the lease some time prior to the expiration of the lease. We don't want to wait till the morning after the lease expires to look for contractors to rehabilitate the space and to start advertising for a tenant. With some preplanning and anticipation, we can turn the space around and replace the tenant with a minimal lapse of rental income.

As we create each new lease, we note on our long-term calendar not only the *escalation* and *expiration* dates, but the date that the tenant is required by the lease to notify us of intent either to vacate or to extend the lease.

C.P.I.   The index is published at the end of *odd* months, covering the two-month period ending with the last *even* month. We calendar anniversary dates of leases containing escalator clauses, so that by the time the clause may be put into effect we can perform the computation of the new, escalated rent and give the tenant time to put the rent increase through their payables system.

Insurance Coverage.   Within our chronology segment, a big item is insurance. We usually require our tenants to carry insurance and name us as *additional loss payables* on their policy, so that their agent or carrier has to notify us in the case of a change or any suspension of coverage.

The insurance inception and expiration dates seldom track the tenant's lease dates, so we use our calendar to trigger a call to the tenant if no certificate shows up indicating that the policy has been renewed.

The Physical Plant.   It might be appropriate to remind the reader that the building was the star of the text for many pages before we strayed into this jungle of accounting and lease verbiage.

The final comment under the science of utilizing a long-term calendar productively is to key maintenance events and warranties into your calendar system. A product with a multiyear shelf life or a facility with an inspection or replacement cycle exceeding one year are candidates for inclusion on the calendar.

We're told that long-term calendars are available, but we've never seen a long-term calendar much better than a loose-leaf binder that we've kept for years, some pages headed by years, with events and dates for that year to be put on the pages of the Day-Timer calendar arriving just before the new year commences.

The trick is not to lose the binder from year to year!

Lease Revenue

Accepting rent from tenants is why we're here, property managers, but there isn't a great deal that need be said about it. In basic terms, we take their check and deposit it. If it's on time, it's of little consequence.

If the check is late, please accept this pointer. A legal doctrine called *laches* obligates one party to a contract to act within a reasonable time to hold the other to an agreed-upon but unfulfilled term of that contract or, eventually, the right to enforce that term if the contract is lost.

Such a term is rent, payable on the first day of the month. According to the doctrine of laches, if a lessor continually accepts rent significantly after that date, at some point the lessor will be unable to find the tenant in breach for a late payment—that tenant can mount a viable defense based on the laches doctrine. In effect, the due date of rent becomes *de facto* adjusted to the usual date on which the tenant paid it and the lessor accepted it.

To combat the chain of events necessary to establish a valid claim against enforcement of delinquent rent penalties, we'll offer an idea to run by your attorney: Our suggestion is for a rubber stamp, with the text "Acceptance of rent on a late basis shall not jeopardize future rights of lessor to enforce rental payment on a timely basis," or words to that effect. What we're saying is that we'll take it this time, but don't make a habit of it. (New federal check-clearing requirements give us less room to write all these things we used to write on the back of tenants' checks, but this should fit on the late check somewhere.)

Nonrent Items.   Some terms of our leases allow or require us to collect some funds in the same form and at the same time rent is due, and nonpayment of such funds are handled in a way similar to delinquent payment or nonpayment of rent, with similar remedies to the lessor, but we receive and account for them differently.

The principal's accountant is a resource to learn of these nonrent collections and we'll not belabor them here, but be prepared to account for items other than rent, such as monthly parking-space rental (which may vary each month), guest parking validation ticket books or blanks used in the parking area's gate, center advertising paid for by the owner and apportioned out to tenants and finally tenant association dues, usually collected like rent and remitted to the association. There are probably other charges.

We mention this to call attention to the fact that each month's total bank deposits, even in small centers and office buildings, usually varies each month and needs reconciliation.

Advance Rent.   This is where our calendar is useful in budgeting rental income: Tenants not exercising options to renew leases are usually eligible to apply their prepaid last month's rent to the final period of the lease.

And a prediction: Many tenants, having met the requirements of a tenant in good standing during the original lease term, might demand that their deposit be credited to the first month of the option period. Or they may not wait that long; in some longer leases a tenant may negotiate a deposit credit at the end of the second year, for example, if all terms of the lease have been met by then. This takes us back to the calendar topic earlier in this chapter—effective calendaring would note a credit in rental income in the 25th month of that tenant's term.

*   *   *   *

We'll not belabor revenue further—obviously the manager is running a business and the precepts of any business apply to the management company's banking practices, record keeping, office procedure and general accounting.

Management Marketing Expenses

The final category of administrative attention by a management company is management expense, which can be a sore point in some management–ownership relations.

A clear duty of property managers is the expenditure of the owner's funds for the predictable expenses of operation—taxes, insurance, maintenance, labor and equipment. This we do, with an eye toward economy and an examination of competitive alternatives wherever possible, and with stringent record keeping. Another duty, paramount in state licensing agencies' eyes, is an accounting of revenues and expenditures, and distribution of any residual funds held in trust for the principal's account.

Less clear are funds spent in leasing activities, intended to draw potential tenants to the property. Many of these funds are speculative and may not result in one particular new lease, at least in a time frame close to the expenditure. We need a firm agreement with our principal about how much of the revenue dollar may be allocated to entertain potential tenants of the premises.

Management Expense Authority.   In a vein similar to the entertainment and marketing expenses above, we need to establish a worst-case-scenario procedure to address some limited and defined instances when the necessity to commit the principal to an expenditure may not wait until dawn.

Most of these cases involve failure of some mechanical equipment or damage to the property, and a prominent qualifier is whether the expenditure is elective or mandatory, and whether covered by insurance or a warranty.

A dollar figure is difficult to establish—we urge a meeting of minds with your principal, well before the emergency develops. Often there's no clear guideline: If the HVAC compressor blows a head in July, it definitely has to be repaired, now. But it may happen at the end of September, when repairs can wait for six months, and we may decide, with the luxury of time to invite bids, to upgrade the system.

A sharp manager, who has discussed such eventualities with a principal many months before and has a clear idea of ownership priorities and objectives, can decide independently of the principal, if he or she's not immediately available, to get the thing fixed or let it ride through autumn. And as time marches on, that manager achieves an increasing threshold of discretionary authority in the operation of the building, and the owner can stay on the beach in Maui, where all owners belong.

The Power of Attorney.   If our principal's across town, a power of attorney is less important than if he or she were in fact on Ka'anapali Beach, but either way the document deserves some consideration. Our management contract, discussed in the Introduction, has a direct bearing on some of the duties that we are charged with, but that document speaks of our relationship with the principal and is not binding upon third parties. The power of attorney is the ticket for filling this void.

Thought varies between the states, management firms, principals and assignments, and we'll leave it to you to determine whether you should have a limited power to conduct effectively the property's business in your principal's stead. We include it here as an element of management that needs consideration.

The Notice of Nonresponsibility.   This is one of those terms that we can't believe is uniform in all the 50 states, but we're unable to find a variation.

The intent of the form is to tell the world that the owner of the property will not be responsible for payment for any goods or services delivered to the property unless a written agreement exists prior to delivery of such goods or services by a vendor or contractor.

We include the legal description and the commonly known address of the property on the form and have the owner of the property execute it with a notary public as witness. We then file the document with the recorder of the county where the *property* is located (not the domicile of the owner) and consider the world notified. A prudent contractor or vendor checks the county records prior to delivering the goods.

The obvious peril is that a tenant, doing work on the premises they rent in the center, contracts for goods and services, doesn't pay the bills, and contractors, absent the Notice of Nonresponsibility, have recourse against the fee owner of the property.

We're writing now of a legal concept, and when we do so we like to advise the reader to consult with an attorney, who is closer to your state laws than we are, for the final good word on the Notice of Nonresponsibility in your area.

Recording the Lease.   Many prudent lessees choose to file with the county recorder a notice that they hold a lease and therefore a personal property interest in real property within the county. There are good technical reasons for doing so, far outside the bounds of this property-management book.

A lease is a cumbersome document to record, primarily due to the page count of many of our leases. The complete lease also usually contains proprietary information that one or both parties don't wish to make a matter of public record.

To accomplish the intent of the parties, we record an *abstract* of the lease—an encapsulation offering the public the legal and common description of the property and the parties to and duration of the contract. That information is sufficient to disclose the existence of the lease in fairly certain terms, while keeping the balance of the language privileged.

Small-property managers frequently aren't affected by these documents, but an increasing number of chain and franchise tenants want their leases recorded. Your principal's attorney, who should review all your contracts anyway, can hammer out an abstract for the tenant to file if they so choose.

*   *   *   *

That last line offers a clue about the next chapter. From the way we've written about our task to this point, one might surmise that only three people were involved in the management business: the manager, a tenant and the owner.

There are many more people who make the job easier or more difficult, more or less enjoyable and definitely more profitable. We'll meet some of them now.

14

Liaison

One of the least predictable liaisons that property managers perpetu-
ate is that with the news media—sometimes to plug the center, other
times to respond to incidents occurring on the property. The most fa-
mous media stunt to date is the Thanksgiving bombing of a Cincin-
nati shopping center with live turkeys from the WKRP helicopter.

In a small town in the foothills near Reno, a center owner worked
the weekly paper like Heifetz worked a Stradivarius. He invited the
cowboys recreating the annual wagon-train crossing of the Sierra to
use the center's parking lot for the grub-stop barbecue.

The paper carried a photo of the event, or rather its aftermath in-
cluding evidence of a hundred oxen, draught horses and donkeys.

Free publicity is not always sweet. Or fragrant.

*   *   *   *

Bearing in mind that we've already established that the owner of this
little piece of the rock that we've been managing for the last dozen-
odd chapters is basking in the sun on a beach in Hawaii, the responsibility of dealing with a rather broad assortment of people falls upon
us. This is not a chapter promising deep narrative explanations, as
most of it is obvious. What we are trying to provide is food for
thought, with the underlying intent that some of the thoughts might
inspire you to clear certain decisions and options with your principal
prior to his or her takeoff for the 50th state.

We've categorized these people. Now let's try to get acquainted with them.

The Owner's Other Agents

Assuming that the property has "absentee ownership"—an owner or entity located away from your town—or that your owner spends a good part of time out of town, we need to know the other people who undertake responsibilities for the same ownership.

We include among these people an *attorney*, who we'll call fairly frequently as legal issues arise within the building, as leases are created or when tenants fall into delinquency and management responsibilities cross into the legal realm.

From time to time we will be in a position to expend money on behalf of the owner, and the *accountant* should be included in that decision—to expend this tax year or to wait a year, and whether to categorize the expenditure as maintenance or capitalization.

Our experience has been that by maintaining close contact and having a fairly cordial relationship with these professionals, we are able to leave the owner pretty much undisturbed, and talk among ourselves to a point that when we *do* call the owner for instructions, we are able to offer a number of options, sparing the owner the necessity of consultation with the attorney and accountant prior to making a decision.

Insurance

The process of keeping the owner's insurance current in appropriate limits of coverage, and interfacing building insurance with that carried by the tenants, can take up a great deal of time. You'll soon note that a new tenancy creates a flurry of phone calls, from the building insurors and those of the new tenant.

Given a choice, we like to communicate directly with the new tenant's insurance agent, in order to communicate limits of liability, the correct name and address of the additional loss payable (your owner) and the inception and expiration dates of the policy. If the tenants plan some endeavor where an out-of-the-ordinary coverage is indicated, we might have their agent call our agent and confirm that coverage benefitting both entities is in effect. A strong element in our prelease conversation with new tenants includes the name of their agent, with a request that he or she call us early after the lease is signed.

The Field Underwriters.   Please note there are local insurance *agents,* designated by an insuring *company,* who sell the insurance coverage and transmit the specifications of the coverage to that company.

That company, frequently not in the same town as your building, gives the information to an *underwriter* who evaluates the risk. That person may have specific questions, and those questions are given to the *field underwriter,* who journeys to your town and seeks you out.

These fieldmen (as they're known in the industry) may be sent by the insuror covering the *building* or by the insuror covering the *tenant.* In either case, they have questions that may be related to fire, to "inland marine" coverage (burglary, theft, illegal entry) or to third-party liability (steps, handrails, night lighting and life safety).

Most managers agree that a significant amount of time is spent with the insurance fieldmen in office or retail centers. It's productive time—our properties are the better for their involvement, and they get their information straight from the horse's mouth, the nag most conversant with the property.

Insurance Adjustors.   The last segment mentioned a few coverages: fire and extended coverage, theft, burglary and liability. We'll add a few: products and completed operations, insuring exactly those; plate glass, covering large windows and doors; and customer's goods floaters, insuring the merchant for loss of the property of others while in the care, custody and control of that merchant; and we're starting to sound like a textbook.

The thrust of the words is that in a busy center or office, claims occur with some regularity for one of these perils, and like as not the ownership of the building is brought into the fray. You, Mr. or Ms. Manager, will assist the adjustors sent by the insurance carrier(s) in sorting out these problems.

The Insurance Rate Bureau.   Our final guest on the premises from the insurance industry is a fairly frequent visitor also—the person from the "bureau."

The bureau, to old-time insurance people (are there any other kind?), is the independent body paid by the insurance companies to assess the degree of risk present in a building, as a baseline to establish the cost of insuring that building against a number of perils. We worked for Hartford Insurance about the time the Fab Four hit America's shores, and our duties with sprinklered risks kept us close to the *Pacific Fire Rating Bureau,* a West Coast entity that became known in later years nationally as the *Insurance Service Office* (usually just the ISO). It is still called the bureau by most insurance people.

You'll hear periodically from the ISO—usually whenever a tenant that raises the risk moves in, e.g., a dry cleaner with flammable chemicals; or when any remodeling is undertaken. The trigger may be a building permit or a new business license. Like the company fieldman, the person from the bureau is on our side. Time spent with these field personnel is productive, and you'll spend quite a bit of it.

Public Safety

This segment could drag out forever, but we needn't do that to a reader. The insurance people are less known to those new in the property-management field and needed some embellishment. But the municipal police, fire, public health, traffic and building-safety agencies should be well known already, so suffice it to say that we should maintain a high degree of availability to each of those agencies' personnel.

We like to offer each of them our card so that we may be located in a hurry if necessary. And most honor our request to keep us apprised of occurrences, correspondence and events concerning our building. If the health department receives a complaint about one of our tenants, or if the police must be called to calm down a donnybrook in the tavern in our center, we'd like to hear about it.

Most of our leases require some adherence to public policy and ordinances, and if enforcement agencies are making frequent trips to our building, we may be entitled under the lease to revise our tenant list.

Neighbors

Assuming some sort of homogeneous development in your town, your retail center is probably close to other retail centers, as is your office building.

Within the safety-in-numbers theory—otherwise, might-makes-right—it's nice to keep the lanes of communication open with our neighbors, for the good of the building ownership and the tenants. Exterior factors affecting them probably affect us also, and a consensus is nice when approaching a municipal body or traffic agency, an enforcement agency or a trade association, for redress from some problem.

Even in the absence of a problem, it's just good business to help out neighboring tenants and buildings, and your management office usually provides the point of commonality for all your tenants' input into issues affecting their businesses.

Civic Affairs

From time to time, the building needs a ceremonial figurehead to represent the tenancy and ownership at some solemn occasions—the opening of a new street comes to mind as a recent example—and an adjoining shopping center was asked to provide a representative to the proceedings. We'd probably delegate that to a tenant with a gift of gab, but he or she might send it back to us, so that's a task to add to your list of management duties.

Closely aligned with this is a donation of space in the center to a public service group for a nonprofit use, and allowing the tenants within the center to bask in the glow of the goodwill the donation creates. The topic's been covered previously, in the "Common Areas" chapter, but we include it here because the people who seek out these donated facilities are frequent guests in our office. Such a program should be done under the aegis of the owner, and with input from the accountant, who may be able to impute such use as a charitable donation by the owner.

The Media

Wonderful things happen in or around our properties, and to people who work in them, and readers haven't really joined the property-management community until a TV reporter levels a floodlamp at them at two o'clock in the morning and asks whether the fire in the furnace room will have any significant effect on the tenants' Christmas party tomorrow.

The time to meet the press is before things go awry, and their membership should be treated as a resource. Often we are able to change the short-term course of our property by properly couching a response or by guiding favorable news attention toward a tenant.

Press releases are a valuable tool for property managers, and most media seek news as vigorously as we seek media exposure. Most local press associations have periodic workshops on media relations for community businesspeople—we highly endorse these.

Resist the urge to feed the TV reporter his camera—you'll lose, every time; just ask Sean Penn!

The Real Estate Broker

This professional is an ongoing presence in our properties, unless they are chock-full of tenants and we are never advertising to fill vacancies.

In days gone by, a real estate broker might bring us an acceptable prospective tenant, and to compensate that broker we apportioned a part of that tenant's rent to the broker for a period of months or paid a fee up front.

The rules are changing; *buyer agency* spills over into commercial rentals, and it's possible that the new tenant is paying that broker's fee for locating the premises.

In the longer run, it matters not who is paying the fee—we want to treat real estate brokers and salespeople with courtesy, professionalism and with an eye to the National Association of REALTORS® Code of Ethics. Concurrently, we are agents of a principal, with an obligation of obedience to their wishes.

Cooperation with and the compensation of a licensed real estate broker as a subagent to secure leases is a hot topic to discuss with your principal—you're bound by his or her convictions, whether or not they align with your own. No opinions are voiced here, aside from mentioning that as a REALTOR® we believe in the profession and our collective expertise, consistent with adherence to fiduciary relationships and making sure we know who's paying whose fee.

*   *   *   *

And that, fellow managers, adds a few characters to the cast of our profession.

Now—the proof of the pudding—let's go take over a new building account!

15

Setting Up a New Account

Just as the envelope with the eagle, the scales of justice and the jury commissioner's return address seldom encloses news that we've been excused from jury duty for life, we find that we're seldom chosen to assume responsibility for a commercial building because the last manager was doing such a bang-up job and things are running so smoothly.

In truth, the typical building owner often keeps a failing manager well past the time when he or she should have been terminated, and we arrive on a scene that would be better managed by a cross between Houdini and Harry Callahan.

* .* * *

So here we go into a new account, with neither a rabbit in our hat nor a magnum on our hip. We'll start by taking an inventory of existing leases and other promises exchanged between the owner and the tenants and move on to an evaluation of the physical plant, personal property and building maintenance records. The information we'll develop will serve as a baseline for the activities necessary to carry out our employer's ownership goals.

But don't get restless with the text, if you're in the happy situation of starting off fresh as the first manager of a brand-new building. The words that follow will keep you from becoming the manager that Dirty Harry has to clean up after in the years to come.

Lease/Tenant Correlation

The initial effort is two-pronged: The first action is to walk the building, be it a retail center or an office, noting the name on each and every sign, lobby directory, freight door, parking space or anywhere else a name appears. And don't overlook the more subtle *de facto* leases: telephone booths, billboards on standards in the parking lot, bus benches, vending machines in the common area and signs advertising an off-premises business down the street. All of these in the latter category put revenue in someone's pocket, and that pocket should probably rightfully be your principal's.

Document Inventory

The second prong of this early effort is a gathering of every piece of paper the departing manager left behind that could be held out to create a leasehold interest or some form of license or permission for a party or object to remain on the property.

These documents should be critiqued as soon as possible with attention paid to the term and currency of the agreement, the path of revenue that the document creates and the conformance of the agreement to the actual use of the property. The small poster allowed in an agreement occasionally swells to a pylon-mounted billboard if nobody's watching!

The fun begins as we start matching the occupant of a store to a current lease, or a phone booth to an agreement with the utility company. Ideally we'll wind up with a one-for-one match and run out of leases and agreements just as we cross out the last item on the physical inventory list.

And the Edsel will make a triumphant return to showrooms, the temporary victim of a minor marketing oversight.

More probably, we'll have a document left over without an occupant or a vending machine to match, or we'll find a newspaper vending rack but no agreement with the distributor. All these orphans go in a stack, to be dealt with when time permits. And since revenue is involved, sooner is better.

*   *   *   *

If we were to prioritize activities at this juncture, we'd probably first address the occupant of an office or retail bay with no apparent lease—it sounds far-fetched that this could occur, but occur it has, and remember it's possible that you didn't get this account because diligence was recently abounding. Hopefully you inherited a set of books, and the occupant's presence will get scarier yet if rent has not been coming in on that space. If rent *is* being generated, you have more a paper problem than a trespasser-in-tenancy.

With those obvious detractions to revenue put into proportion, we move onto the leases, and particularly to the acceleration clauses they contain. The comparison here is the rent apparently being collected versus what the lease indicates the current rent to be. If you can't kick the property's overall income up by 5 percent in a retail center by paying attention to what the last manager let slide, you probably need new batteries in your calculator.

Next in line are the on-site gadgets that someone is making money from: If no agreements turn up relating to the sign or the phone booth, a call to the apparent owners with a request to supply the agreement or remove the property will usually produce the agreement. And some revenue should be showing up in the prior deposit slips.

Bear in mind that some fixtures probably generate no rent but have been placed as traffic generators or conveniences to tenants, e.g., a Federal Express pick-up box. But even those should be supported by an agreement with the owner.

The Questionnaire

Right about now the tenants (or trespassers!) begin to get the message that there's a new sheriff in town, and at some point early after your arrival you'll benefit by circulating a rumor-squelching newsletter announcing your arrival, phone number and intentions. You'll be pleased to know that a new management team is usually a welcome breath of fresh air in most centers, if in fact you're replacing a less-than-effective entity.

We suggest a questionnaire along the lines of "This is your retail center/office building—how may we make it a better place to shop/work?" A second query is arguably more important: "What verbal representations have been made to you that you are presently relying on?" We thereby make it incumbent upon the tenant to reveal his or her interpretation of a prior manager's agreement, and if no verbal agreements are cited when this opportunity is presented, we're in a stronger position down the road to deal with the "so-and-so always (fill in the blank)": accepted late rent, let me park there, washed our windows, whatever. Solicit the questionnaires and retain them.

The Paper Factory

Concurrent with the above shaking-out activities, we'll suggest two other efforts that should be underway during this first 30-day start-up period. One effort is the physical plant evaluation we undertook at the beginning of this chapter. The second is a look at the paperwork that serves as the foundation under the management of all commercial buildings. In most management circumstances, administration of these responsibilities falls within your contract.

Insurance

We mentioned the *people* involved in the insurance process earlier—now we have to confirm the existing *coverages*. Two categories of hazard insurance are paramount here. The first is the coverage of the physical structure itself, coverage that would rebuild the structure after a loss from a named peril and provide the owner with proceeds in lieu of lost rental income while the building is being rebuilt. This is usually part of a package policy that includes third-party liability and personal injury (libel, slander, defamation of character and false eviction). You might also check to see to what extent that insurance covers *you*, while working in the owner's behalf.

A second category of insurance of interest to a building manager is insurance carried by the building tenants, usually mandated by lease agreement. In some circles it's known as OL&T coverage—Owner, Landlord and Tenant. The policy form includes named perils (damages occasioned to your building by the tenant), and it includes liability to protect the owner against claims made by persons injured while doing business in the building through the fault of the tenant.

These policies should name the owner as an additional insured or loss payable, and we'll leave it to your insurance agent to explain that semantic difference. An important duty in tenant insurance matters is the calendaring system of the "Administration" chapter, to ensure that coverages are sufficient and renewed as they expire. (Lapse or cancellation of the policy automatically results in the owner, if named as additional insured, being notified.)

Periodic Responsibilities

A remarkable number of elements within our new responsibility are subject to a mandatory or optional form of activity every so often, and another early ''set-up'' effort is to integrate this new account into your calendaring system.

Consider elevators, boilers and fire sprinklers, which require by statute an annual or semiannual inspection. For those, the inspectors call us, but other requirements, such as pumping a restaurant grease trap, usually have to be initiated by the building manager. HVAC equipment needs periodic filter service, lubrication and flame-height adjustment; emergency generators and sprinkler air compressors need a tune-up. And twice a year, we get to reset the clocks, HVAC setbacks, outside lights, gates and sprinkler systems to or from daylight savings time!

If you've inherited a workable log from your predecessor, you're in good shape. But if not, a comprehensive list of periodic obligations transferred to a calendar will make life flow a lot easier.

Trust Funds

What we're primarily addressing in this category are funds held by the owner or prior manager as advance rental deposits (or cleaning deposits, rare in commercial rentals but prevalent in apartments). In all truth, the best time to reconcile the trust fund balance with the owner is prior to the time you accept money into your trust.

In practice, you may assume that most of the tenants in your 12-unit retail center tendered a deposit, frequently the equivalent of a month's rent at the time they executed a lease and took possession. And we'll say the rents are $500 a month. In a perfect world, you would mathematically inherit a $6,000 trust fund, and as each tenant eventually gave notice to vacate, you could transfer $500 from your trust account to your operating account, or in simple terms, give that tenant the last month free.

That naiveté is of the sort that expects the return of the Edsel to the showroom, and we offer to wager the price on the dust jacket of this book that of the 12 tenants, a few have no rent prepaid, some still owe a part of the $500 and at least one with shaky credit paid two months in advance—and that the balance in the account is not $6,000.

What you have in your trust account is 12 little time bombs, set to go off as each tenant vacates, or to be perpetuated when they extend their lease. And the fuses on some run out to three, four or even ten years—the life of each lease. Other deposits may be credited as rent upon some lease anniversary; we know a landlord, a real fun guy who wants two months up front prepaid and then gives the tenant the 13th and the 25th month free if they're still in good standing (on a three-year lease).

Without beating a point to death, what we want to do, early in our new association with the project, is to verify the trust fund balance by comparing the apparent balance to the terms in the individual leases, and if the balances receipted on the leases don't add to the trust fund's balance, we want to find out why. For sure, we'll balance it now, or we'll balance it later when the tenant is vacating, but balance it we will, and the passage of time only clouds the issue further.

This effort obviously nudges up to the boundary between real estate management and accounting, and in truth it might be closer to an accounting function, but in your new building you'll frequently be working with your owner's accounting firm, and a trust-account reconciliation is a good way to get the relationship rolling.

Personal Property

In the normal course of events, a management firm may from time to time purchase durable goods and consumable supplies that we need to carry out the management function. In our own experience, we buy durable goods that we use for all our projects as a group, e.g., hand tools to keep on the truck and office furnishing and equipment for our own office. We pay for them from the office operating account as a cost of doing business and that's that.

But we buy other durable supplies specifically for one project, and those supplies benefit that project alone. Our usual employment contracts empower us to purchase supplies from time to time and present the owner/principal with the bills for reimbursement.

We take some pride in being accountable for the durable hardware we spend our principal's money on, be it a dozen Master padlocks at $6 apiece or a $1200 John Deere snowblower. If we later turn over the management to you, we want to have 12 locks hanging on shackles somewhere on the property and the snowblower parked in the maintenance shed. And everything else—from shovels and sweepers to extention ladders and exercise equipment—in place, marked with a distinctive decal or engraving.

We're driving home a double-edged message: If you as a manager buy an item, ranging in value from an entry door mat or a Rubbermaid trash can to a riding mower or a "cherry picker" lift, keep track of it and ensure that your successor assumes custody of it. If you're on the other end, as the successor taking over an account, determine early in the relationship what personal property your new owner/principal's records show to be on site, and confirm that all that property you're now responsible for is on the premises.

The Vendors and Repairers

A list of those who have worked on the building before we managed it is the final area for a little research as this new account takes its place with our other responsibilities. One of the first tasks is to decide who among them we want to retain.

The basic crafts are obvious: the plumber, the electrician, glazers, painters, HVAC repairers and a general contractor who can get the maintenance and minor remodeling jobs done. If they've been upholding their responsibilities for a reasonable charge, we welcome them back aboard, preferably with written notice advising them of our arrival, our expectations and our billing/accounts payable procedures. Often a touchy issue at this juncture is the bills that vendors have presented to prior management and have not been paid, and parts and services that were ordered or authorized by prior management but not yet delivered. (A related issue is filing the Notice of Nonresponsibility—see the "Administration" chapter.)

We've no solution for those issues—we mention them as areas to investigate and settle on a case basis early in your tenure.

*   *   *   *

Attention to these pointers in a chapter that starts a new account and nearly finishes a book, coupled with the balance of the book, should get you off to a running start managing the local 12-bay retail center and the two-story office building that we focused on as examples so many pages ago.

We come now to the same fork in the text that we've stood at in several books prior to this one: The path to the one side says that if some words are good, more are better; the more inviting path reminds us to quit while we're still ahead. Our goal has been a lay-language treatment of mainstream small-to-moderate-size retail and office properties, such as all of us find in our own towns.

We placed into those buildings tenants that each of us would expect to lease to, and subjected those tenants and ourselves to situations that arise, if not every day, at least once a year or during the life of every leasing period. We think our treatment is adequate preparation for those normal management dilemmas; further inclusion of specialized buildings and unusual tenancies presenting once-in-a-career problems only bog down the text. You'll land in such a quandary of your own early in your management tenure, and you can tell us how you solved it. When you're pioneering uncharted territory, you and your own wits become the only expert in town!

This show's about over, and as the house lights come back up, we'll issue a wish for good luck in your management endeavors. Our paths may cross again—we admit now that we planned this book to include apartment/condominium management side-by-side with commercial leaseholds, and we learned very early in the manuscript that writing about where people work and where they live in the same book is cumbersome for thee and me. A short epilogue puts that into perspective.

Epilogue

Commercial and Residential Management, Two Different Disciplines

Gather around, property managers, and slip on your sensible shoes. We're going to take a walking tour of a large city, and then share a few final thoughts as we stroll out of the pages of this book.

It's a Saturday or Sunday, a morning or an afternoon, and we're in the core of a downtown business district. In our favorite big city (you can pick your own!), we're on streets named Sansome, Montgomery, Kearney and Sacramento, lined by high rises with *Alcoa, Standard Oil, Southern Pacific Railroad* and *The Bank of America* on their facades. The *Transamerica* Pyramid towers over them all—so many tall buildings that sunlight hits these streets for only a few hours each day. Yes, we picked San Francisco.

And there isn't a living soul on the streets. The only sounds are the cars rolling high above on the Bay Bridge, the bell on a cable car crossing Grant Avenue in Chinatown and the foghorn on Alcatraz. A thousand street-level parking spaces sit empty, ten thousand more in basements below the buildings await Monday-morning motorists. The delis and magazine shops are shuttered. Whether it be the multi-million-dollar tower owned by Levi Strauss or the newsstand on Market Street—both lie fallow and unproductive on this weekend.

* * * *

The people and the cars and the kids and the puppies are blocks away, in the William Henry Dana tower, or several Hills away: Nob, Russian or Cathedral. But the billions of dollars' worth of unoccupied struc-

171

tures in the Financial District still need police and fire protection. And minimum heat and light. And the dozens of municipal buses that plied the streets Friday afternoon languish in the car barn this weekend. We've heard all this expounded before, but it took our walk downtown to reach this vacant Orwellian setting and realize that *Americans don't live where they work.*

*   *   *   *

Right-thinking and forward-looking types see a day in the coming millennium when our towns will locate shops, theaters and restaurants on the street levels of our buildings; we'll work in the middle floors of the building by day and we'll go home to the upper stories at night. The streets will be busy all week, the parking levels will be utilized to the maximum, bus lines will find passengers on the corner every day and our rock, in general, will have people enjoying *all* of it, *all* the time. This arrangement is not far in the future—it's starting to happen in major cities and will make for a dandy property-management book as this trend solidifies.

And this concept isn't exactly a reinvention of the wheel—the earliest European merchants usually lived over their stores!

There's a Point Here Somewhere

After many an hour in classrooms on both sides of the instructor's podium, we reached the conclusion that teaching and learning should be fun things to do, and usually remain so until some stuffed shirt comes along and makes hard work of them. Consequently, we write books as if we're all just sitting around the campfire, swappin' a few yarns about real estate or property management.

But in spite of the apparent informality, we *do* start with a framework that gets filled in and fleshed out—and realigned and augmented if facts change while the work is in progress—until the original framework and the finished work could easily be mistaken for two different books.

We noticed early on that we became continually perplexed while trying to articulate retail/mercantile and office/professional with residential property management. We could treat differences between retail and office leaseholds within a given topic, but the residential aspect of the same topic remained an ongoing dilemma.

A friend clarified the problem: The thread of the term *property management* is not strong enough to bond the two types of property usage together in one book. That problem is analogous to writing about feet in a book about hearts under the justification that a podiatrist and a cardiologist are both *surgeons*.

The parallels are that buildings, retail and office or residential, are all built of sticks and stones and therefore have recognizable similarities in the structural chapters. That idea has some merit, but considerable differences still exist between the two. We might use one thermostat in ten thousand feet of office space but ten separate stats and furnaces in an apartment building of a similar size. Heavy electrical services are localized in a commercial building but fan out to all residential units to run ovens and air conditioners. Similarly we specify vacuum-flush commodes and handicapped-accessible fixtures in commercial buildings, but standard fixtures in residential construction. We shower and wash clothes in the residential setting—the largest water heater in most commercial buildings fits under a bathroom cabinet. Sound-attentuation walls are different. Common areas are also different: model railroad exhibits appear in the marketplace but swing sets are more to the point in the condos and apartments. Office buildings have community photocopy, fax and mail-handling rooms—residential buildings replace them with laundry rooms; the hours of use, plumbing and supply-vending machines for the two installations are again different.

Swing sets suggests a difference of priorities in residential properties—a volume could be written about children and emerging legislation to prevent discrimination against children. Further, how do we handle pets, weekend visitors and waterbeds?—three topics that seldom cause a managerial problem in commercial properties.

Residential and commercial leases differ, in rights of the parties, trade fixtures, escalation and C.P.I. adjustment and the several states' statutes speaking to breach. A book on residential management would probably contain other chapters: discrimination in its many forms, senior-only complexes, units adapted for the disabled and subsidized housing for low-income families.

One of the more interesting aspects of residential management that we look forward to writing about is *density housing occupied by an owner*—a windy way to express *condominium, cooperative apart-*

ment, *town home* and *Planned Unit Development* housing. These are some of the more lucrative fields in the management industry, and a veritable trove of information should be conveyed about them to a reader.

The Human Factor

Little was said throughout the book about the human propensities of the people who inhabit our buildings, but most of us have borne witness to this truth: Other than those working in a building that they own, maintain, pay taxes on and insure, few of us take a deep abiding interest in our workplace. We care to a degree and we try to help our landlords along, but the building is basically someone else's and our interest is temporal.

But: Follow those same Americans home, to an apartment or townhouse that they rent, and watch their roots sink to bedrock and their Yankee blood boil when some dark outside force, which may or may not be the landlord, inhibits or alters the use and possession of rented premises to their perceived detriment. A person's home is traditionally their castle, whether they hold a deed or a lease in the strongbox.

That's our national heritage, and we're grateful that we all can enjoy it.

*   *   *   *

The very existence of that freedom sinks the wedge deeper while writing about management. There are ten-story buildings and homes stacked ten stories high. There are buildings full of offices and towers full of residents. A world of difference exists between the terms of each pair.

We're saving the residential notes, and there are a lot of them. We began this book on a dark and stormy night, and the final words were typed on a glorious Indian summer evening. But when the nights again turn dark and stormy, we might buy a new typewriter ribbon, a fresh gallon of white-out, and strike out again, on the topic of residential management.

We look forward to going home sometime in the future and curling up with the writing of a good residential management book. We hope you'll join us!

Index

Place your order today: Call toll-free 1-800-621-9621, ext. 650.
In Illinois call 312-836-4400, ext. 650. Please mention code 830318.
Or fill out and mail this order form.

Real Estate Education Company / 520 N. Dearborn St. / Chicago, IL 60610-4354

☐ Payment Enclosed

Charge to: ☐ VISA ☐ MasterCard

Account No. _____

Exp. Date _____

Signature _____
(All charge orders must be signed.)

Name _____

Company _____

Street Address _____

City _____ State _____ ZIP _____

Daytime Phone (   ) _____

Return Address:

_____

_____

_____

Place
Stamp
Here

Real Estate
Education Company
Order Department
520 North Dearborn Street
Chicago, Illinois 60610-4354

IMPORTANT—PLEASE FOLD OVER—PLEASE TAPE BEFORE MAILING

NOTE: This page, when folded over and taped, becomes an envelope, which has been approved by the United States Postal Service. It is provided for your convenience.

IMPORTANT—PLEASE FOLD OVER—PLEASE TAPE BEFORE MAILING

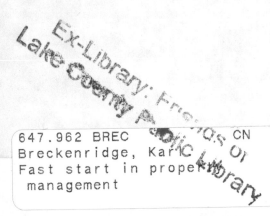